God of Dirt

Mary Oliver and the
Other Book of God

Thomas W. Mann

A Cowley Publications Book

Lanham, Chicago, New York, Toronto, and Plymouth, UK

Published in the United States of America by Cowley Publications, a division of the Society of Saint John the Evangelist. No portion of this book may be reproduced, stored in or introduced into a retrieval system, or transmitted, in any form or by any means—including photocopying—without the prior written permission of Cowley Publications, except in the case of brief quotations embedded in critical articles and reviews.

Library of Congress Cataloging-in-Publication Data:

Mann, Thomas W. (Thomas Wingate), 1944–
   The God of dirt : Mary Oliver and the other book of God / Thomas W. Mann.
      p. cm.
   Includes bibliographical references (p.   ).
   ISBN: 978-1-56101-261-9

1. Oliver, Mary, 1935—Criticism and interpretation. 2. Religion in literature. 3. Nature in literature. 4. God in literature. I. Title.
PS3565.L5Z77 2004
811'.54—dc22

                              2004007167

Unless otherwise indicated, scripture quotations are taken from *The New Revised Standard Version* of the Bible, © 1989, by the Division of Christian Education of the National Council of the Churches of Christ in the United States of America. Used by permission.

From *Winter Hours: Prose, Prose Poems and Poems* by Mary Oliver. Copyright © 1999 by Mary Oliver. Reprinted by permission of Houghton Mifflin Company. All rights reserved.

Excerpts from "Yes! No!", "Blue Heron" and "Roses" from *White Pine: Poems and Prose Poems*, copyright © 1994 by Mary Oliver, reprinted by permission of Harcourt, Inc.

From *Twelve Moons* by Mary Oliver. Copyright © 1972, 1973, 1974, 1976, 1977, 1978, 1979 by Mary Oliver. By permission of Little, Brown and Company, (Inc.).

From *American Primitive* by Mary Oliver. Copyright © 1978, 1979, 1980, 1981, 1982, 1983 by Mary Oliver. By permission of Little, Brown and Company, (Inc.).

From *The Leaf and the Cloud* by Mary Oliver. Copyright © 2000 by Mary Oliver. Reprinted by permission of Perseus Books PLC, a member of Perseus Books, L.L.C.

Books, L.L.C.

From *House of Light* by Mary Oliver. Copyright © 1990 by Mary Oliver. Reprinted by permission of Beacon Press, Boston.

From *New and Selected Poems* by Mary Oliver. Copyright © 1992 by Mary Oliver. Reprinted by permission of Beacon Press, Boston.

From *West Wind: Poems and Prose Poems* by Mary Oliver. Copyright © 1997 by Mary Oliver. Reprinted by permission of Houghton Mifflin Company. All rights reserved.

From *Dreamwork* by Mary Oliver. Copyright © 1986 by Mary Oliver. Used by permission of Grove/Atlantic, Inc. and the author.

Cover design Jennifer Hopcroft.

This book was printed in the United States of America on acid-free paper.

A Cowley Publications Book
Published by Rowman & Littlefield Publishers, Inc.
A wholly owned subsidiary of
The Rowman & Littlefield Publishing Group, Inc.
4501 Forbes Boulevard, Suite 200, Lanham, Maryland 20706
http://www.rowmanlittlefield.com

Estover Road, Plymouth PL6 7PY, United Kingdom

Distributed by National Book Network

For Connie
Thirty-five years of Constancy

"Out of the dirt of the earth Yhwh God shaped the Earthling,
and blew into his nostrils the breath of life,
and the Earthling became a living creature . . .
out of the earth, every tree . . .
out of the earth, every animal and bird."
(Genesis 2.8, 9, 19; author's translation)

CONTENTS

Quotations and other references to Mary Oliver's work are cited in the text with the abbreviations listed below.

AP   *American Primitive.* (Boston: Little, Brown and Co., 1983)
BP   *Blue Pastures.* (New York: Harcourt Brace and Co., 1991)
DW   *Dream Work.* (Boston: The Atlantic Monthly Press, 1986)
HL   *House of Light.* (Boston: Beacon Press, 1990)
LC   *The Leaf and the Cloud.* (New York: Da Capo Press, 2000)
NSP   *New and Selected Poems.* (Boston: Beacon Press, 1992)
OF   *Owls and Other Fantasies.* (Boston: Beacon Press, 2003)
TM   *Twelve Moons.* (Boston: Little, Brown and Co., 1979)
WH   *Winter Hours.* (Boston: Houghton Mifflin Co., 1999)
WK   *What Do We Know.* (New York: Da Capo Press, 2002)
WP   *White Pine.* (New York: Harcourt Brace and Co., 1991)
WW   *West Wind.* (Boston: Houghton Mifflin Co., 1997)

I WAS A COLLEGE STUDENT raised in a rather typical Southern Baptist Church when I first encountered the study of religion as an academic discipline. At the time, I paid little attention to the place of nature in religious traditions, a disregard reflected in the books that I read and lectures that I attended. The civil rights movement was entering its heyday; students were marching and people in the Church were listening to the cries of the oppressed, but no one would have thought to write a book entitled *Listen to the Crying of the Earth*. It would be thirty years before that book appeared.[1] My unexceptional church upbringing did little to fill the gap in appreciating nature spiritually. I sang along with everyone else, "were the whole realm of nature mine, that were a present far too small," and thought nothing of it.

I quickly focused my academic study of religion in the Old Testament, and, when nature was mentioned at all, it was usually negatively. Scholars praised the "mighty acts of God in history" and contrasted them with the "nature religion" of Canaan. The God of ancient Israel was revealed in historical events like the Exodus; the gods of the Canaanites were merely primitive deifications of the forces of nature, their relative insignificance reflected in the lowercase spelling of "gods." Moreover, such nature religion suffered an even greater disrespect, for its devotees allegedly celebrated it in "fertility cults." That was the final straw for decent religious folk, some of whom even looked at dancing with suspicion.

Much has changed in both academia and the religious community. Not only do we now have many books like *Listen to the Crying of the Earth*, but we also have many church and synagogue curricula with titles like *How Do We Care for God's Creation?*[2] There are college courses on ecology, and some divinity schools and seminaries offer courses on "creation spirituality." In addition, people are beginning to pay more attention to a long tradition of "nature writers" as *spiritual* writers, including venerable figures like Henry David Thoreau and John Muir, as well as contemporary writers like Wendell Berry, Gary Snyder, and Annie Dillard. This book seeks to fill a gap by connecting the work of one particular poet, Mary Oliver, with religious and mythological traditions in the Hebrew Bible and other ancient sources.

Studies of the significance of nature in the Bible, often under the rubric of creation, are a helpful corrective to past neglect. However, I contend that the Bible itself simply does not offer us sufficient natural *subjects* (other than human beings) to develop an inclusive natural spirituality. For poets like Oliver, natural subjects are the *primary* subjects. Such poets call our attention to "the grace of the world," to use a phrase of Wendell Berry's.[3] In pointing to this grace, they invite us (whether explicitly or not) to open the "Other Book of God." Theologian Karl Barth once said that theology should be done with the Bible in one hand and the newspaper in the other. Longstanding tradition says that theology (and spiritual growth) can be done with the Bible in one hand and the "book of Nature" in the other. We are about to enjoy the Other Book of God through the eyes of one of its most perceptive and passionate readers.

The writing of a book often is more of a group effort than a solo performance. I am grateful to Michael Wilt of Cowley Publications, without whose interest and persistence this book would not have appeared. I thank Wilda Dockery Boatwright for giving me two of Oliver's books, gifts that led to this one, and I thank Anne Herndon for introducing me to the work of David Abram. I am grateful to a number of people who took the time to read the manuscript in some stage and offer helpful suggestions for improvement: Walter Brueggemann, Ellen Davis, and Candide Jones. Writing requires stretches of uninterrupted time, and I am grateful to the congregation of Parkway United Church of Christ for the summer sabbatical during which I wrote the initial draft (and for listening to innumerable sermons and liturgies laced with Oliver's poems). I thank my parents, who "immersed" me in the water of the ocean, took me camping in the mountains, and forced me to pick beans. I am grateful to my daughter, Mary Liz, my delightful backpacking companion in nature's cathedrals, and to my wife, Connie, who reminds me that there are some things far more important than the writing of books.

WINNER OF THE PULITZER PRIZE for *American Primitive*, Mary Oliver has published eleven books of poetry and four books of essays. Her poems are quoted in everything from Web sites to hymn books. *Earthlight*, a Quaker "Magazine of Spiritual Ecology," has declared her an "earth saint." Although revered by many readers for her spiritual perception of nature, the saint remains largely unnoticed by the scholarly community. In a recent article on her poetry, one interpreter has said that no scholar of religion "has yet given her poetry the sustained attention her work richly deserves."[1]

If we look at religious studies we can easily find a reason that Oliver's work might be neglected. The subject of Oliver's poetry is nature; in addition to people, there are ponds, birds, mammals, reptiles, plants and trees, to name a few. Only with rare exceptions are these *flora* and *fauna* the subjects of religious studies. The omission of natural subjects is understandable because the basic source of Western religion—the Bible—has little regard for them *as subjects with intrinsic spiritual significance*. You will find some glowing descriptions of the natural world as the creation of God, it is true, but the Bible is primarily interested in the *human* subjects who populate its pages. As we shall see, there *are* exceptions to such anthropocentrism, parts of Scripture that invite us to "ask the animals" for instruction (Job 12.7), or to listen to nature's "voice" (Psalm 19). But the historical preoccupation outweighs the natural, and scholarship, until recently, has followed suit. In the last thirty years, however, a growing number of studies have sought to redress the imbalance, to recognize the place of "creation spirituality" within the Bible. Nevertheless, it would be difficult if not impossible to find any studies on the religious significance of an egret, a fawn, or a blackberry vine. A poet who works with such subjects is not a likely candidate for scholarly religious attention.

Another reason that religion scholars might avoid Oliver's work is that she is not a "religious" poet. That is, especially in her earlier poetry, only infrequently does Oliver refer explicitly to God, and sometimes the resulting picture of God is not flattering. The title of this book records an exception, but even here Oliver dares to put the word "god" in lowercase and speaks of a "god of dirt." At the same time, in her poetry human beings do not occupy the exalted status of the "image of God." Instead, we might say that they are "soul brothers and sisters" with all other forms of life, very much a part of what she calls "the family of things." In short, Oliver's theology is sparse at best and often seems heterodox, and her anthropology resembles more that of the "deep ecology" movement than anything recognizably religious.

On the other hand, in her more recent work Oliver refers to or even addresses God more frequently, notably in a praise poem called "*(Matins)*" (WK 51). But even in her earlier poetry, and where there is no reference to God, her poems are undeniably spiritual. Spirituality is an elusive phenomenon, the kind of thing that people often feel that they can recognize and experience even though they can't define it. It is easier to say what it is not than what it is. For many people, spirituality refers to a profound awareness of the deepest meaning of life expressed without any particular religious language, and without any connection to "organized religion." Let us take one line of Oliver's as an example: "the secret name / of every death is life again." It would be difficult to find a pair of words that more generally addresses what it means to be human—indeed, what it means to be part of the world—than life and death. Yet this line of poetry, beautiful in both form and content, uses no explicit religious language, nor does the rest of the poem. Indeed, in my view the poem would be rhymed but utterly ruined if the next line said something like "our life in Jesus, saved from sin." Fortunately, you will never encounter a line like that from Oliver. Moreover, the title of the poem suggests a subject—"Skunk Cabbage"— with which one might not expect to have a "religious experience" (AP 44; NSP 160).

Yet readers who eschew any particular religious affiliation may find her poems strangely evocative of what we normally *call* religious experience. One might in fact define spirituality as religious experience without religious language. Conversely, one might say that religion is nothing else than a formal language used to *name* such an experience, a language that is often, but not necessarily, theistic. Here we must qualify the refusal to call Oliver's poetry "religious." Even when she does not refer to God, she often uses traditionally religious language. She speaks of "souls" and "spirits." She talks of prayer, holiness, and nature's "temple." Her images remind us of priestly blessing, baptism, and sacramental food. She appeals to archetypal themes—light and darkness, alienation and atonement, death and rebirth, including, as in the line above, resurrection. And there are references to both God and Jesus, albeit few and far between.[2] In short, there are enough allusions to religious subjects that her poetry almost seems to *invite* theological interpretation, broadly construed.

One way to understand Oliver's poetry that, I think, recognizes the tension between its spiritual and religious dimensions is to read it as part of "the Other Book of God." The tradition of understanding nature as that other book—alongside the book of Scripture, the Bible—goes back at least to the third century c.e. and St. Anthony the Great (251–356), one of the desert fathers. Once, when a visiting philosopher asked how such a learned man got along in the desert without books, Anthony replied, "My book is the nature of created things, and as often as I have a mind to read the words of God, they are at my hand." Not long after that, St. Augustine (354–430) also identified nature as an alternative scripture:

> Some people, in order to discover God, read books.
> But there is a great book: the very appearance of
> created things. Look above you! Look below you!
> Note it. Read it. God, whom you want to discover,
> never wrote that book with ink. Instead He set
> before your eyes the things that He had made. Can
> you ask for a louder voice than that? What, heaven
> and earth shout to you, "God made me!"[3]

Augustine introduces two critical terms for our subsequent reading of the Other Book of God—"look" and "voice." For God to be revealed someone must be able to see and hear. Clearly, special *ways* of seeing and hearing are involved, a visual and auditory acuity by which the spiritual meaning of nature is discerned. To read adequately the Other Book of God one must have special eyes and ears. On her part, Oliver can refer to this Other Book in a way that makes it *sound* like a Scripture reading: "In the book of the earth it is written" ("Ghosts," *AP* 28; *NSP* 152). She is reading what John Muir called "the divine manuscript."[4]

Among others in the contemporary world, poets often seem to have those eyes and ears for such a reading; they can hear a voice in nature to which others are deaf. One reason for this acuity is the poet's attitude with nature. I say "with" rather than "to" because a poet like Oliver *relates* with nature in such a way that "nature," as an object "out there" to observe, dissolves, and the poet becomes *participant*, someone who is actively "part of" nature rather than "apart from" nature: "Everything is participate" (*LC* 39).[5] Such relational perception often resembles the attitude with nature reflected in the philosophy of language and the anthropology of "primitive" cultures.[6] As we shall see, relational perception, linguistic philosophy, and cultural anthropology all connect in fascinating ways, although we will not be able to explore the connections fully. The correlation appears in the *sensual* way that Oliver *perceives the voice* of nature as the *conversational speech* of a *spiritual family* of which she is an *integral part.*

For those readers of Oliver who appreciate her spirituality but have no interest in religion, I hope they will discover that the correspondence between her poetry and traditional religious language (including Scripture) provides a fresh perspective from which to enjoy her work. For those readers unfamiliar with Oliver—particularly readers who are religious and even members of a religious community—I hope they will discover that Oliver's reading of the Other Book of God invites us into nature's "temple," where we may come into the presence of the holy, and from which we may leave rejuvenated and blessed—in a word, "saved." In particular, I would hope that those within religious communities (church, synagogue, and mosque, to name a few) who have *not* looked at nature as sacred would come to do so, finding that the Other Book of God is just as holy as the "Holy Bible."

I have written this book with a painful awareness of how our culture, including our religious institutions and beliefs, often do *not* see the sacredness of nature. Sadly, Oliver's poetry often has a deeper appreciation for the sanctity of "God's creation" than the very communities who like to use that language. Even more so, Oliver's insistence that we look at nature and see its intrinsic spiritual integrity stands over against the rampant abuse of nature that has brought the world to an environmental crisis. As Roger Rosenblatt has suggested, there is no "concern these days more important than the environment"—not gun control, violence in the media, campaign-finance reform, poverty, war, refugees, and curing fatal diseases.[7]

Before any attempt to address the problems of environmental degradation, however, we must undergo a change of consciousness. We must come to a new sense of the sacredness of the earth under our feet and the sky over our heads. We must come to the humble awareness that we humans are only one part of "the family of things." We must experience a new vision of the beauty of our world. That is why we so desperately need the artists among us.

"I am a performing artist," Oliver says, "I perform admiration. / Come with me, I want my poems to say. And do the same."[8] That is exactly what we intend to do.

•:•

ONE

The Circuit of the Sun: "Earth-talk"

The god of dirt
came up to me many times and said
so many wise and delectable things, I lay
on the grass listening
to his dog voice,
crow voice,
frog voice; *now*,
he said, and *now*,

and never once mentioned *forever*. . . .
(DW 50; NSP 120)

"T HE GOD OF DIRT" emits the strong scent of unorthodoxy, but
also the sweet smell of earth. This, the third stanza of "One
or Two Things," immediately raises questions about the
religious dimensions of Oliver's world. Here there is *a* god, but
one who at first seems unrecognizable, at least to Judeo-Christian
religious tradition. We know of the "God of heaven," and even
the "God of heaven and earth," but a god *of* dirt? What could
such a phrase mean? How does the pronoun "of" function here?
Does it mean that god (to continue Oliver's spelling) is *made* of
dirt? Or does it mean that god is somehow associated with and
characterized by dirt, as in the phrase "a man of principle"? In
other words, is this god an "earthy" character?

What does it mean when Oliver says that this earthy god
"came up" to her and spoke? What kind of speaking is involved
here? Is it what religious discourse calls "revelation"? Then the
agents of that speaking only deepen the weirdness of this god,
who talks with a "dog voice, / crow voice, / frog voice."
Suddenly the "god of dirt" is canine, avian, and reptilian—a god
who barks, chirps, or croaks. Elsewhere the voices become trees

and insects: "Everyday—a little conversation with God, or his envoy / the tall pine, or the grass-swimming cricket" (*LC* 9).

Surely we have now left far behind any traditional (and respectable) notion of God, reverting back to some sort of animism. In a sense, that is true. One of Oliver's books is called *American Primitive*, and much of her poetry explores the world of nature from a "primitive" perspective—that is, from a perspective that we can see in "primitive" peoples. As David Abram puts it, "In indigenous, oral cultures, nature itself is articulate; it speaks. The human voice in an oral culture is always to some extent participant with the voices of wolves, wind, and waves—participant, that is, with the encompassing discourse of an animate earth. . . . Any sound may be a voice, a meaningful utterance."[1] Indeed, Abram's menagerie mirrors Oliver's "dog voice, / crow voice, / frog voice": gurgling frogs, snarling wildcats, honking geese, singing blackbirds.[2]

No doubt some of Oliver's readers will not be able to entertain the notion of a "god of dirt." The "animistic" theological implications will lead them to condemn her poetry as "pagan." That would be most unfortunate, because Oliver is a poet who can open us to another way of seeing the world that is profoundly spiritual, even though often shorn of explicit religious language. Oliver lies there "on the grass listening." Perhaps it is because she is humble enough to "get down to earth" that she can hear the "god of dirt" speaking. Perhaps it is because she will take the time to listen that she can glean the wisdom that this earthy god has to impart. As a poet Oliver is a linguist who hears that most basic language in which we are immersed—"the very voice of the trees, the waves, and the forests," to use the words of one philosopher of language.[3]

What wise things does the "god of dirt" say? What is the nature of this divine wisdom? Attend to what is *now*, rather than pine for what is *forever*. But, as she tells us in the next stanza, "forever" is what has always preoccupied her. What can relieve her of this fixation? In the final stanza, Oliver returns to the image of a butterfly introduced in stanza 2:

> For years and years I struggled
> just to love my life. And then
>
> the butterfly
> rose, weightless, in the wind.
> "Don't love your life

too much," it said,
and vanished
into the world.

The butterfly speaks also. One of the most short-lived of crea-
tures, and one of the most delicate and beautiful, it says that the
poet can love her life so much that real living cannot happen.
The stages of life of a butterfly provide a familiar symbol of incu-
bation and birth. If Oliver evokes that symbolism here, "loving
your life too much" would refer to the cocoon stage. Had the
butterfly longed to stay in its cocoon forever, it would never
have become a butterfly. It would never be "transformed" (liter-
ally "metamorphosed"). The same is true for humans who long
for "forever." As a contemporary proverb puts it, "some people
long for eternal life but don't know what to do on a Sunday
afternoon." The longing for "forever" prevents an enjoyment of
the "now."[4] The hope of vanishing into heaven blocks our enter-
ing "into the world."

The lesson that nature teaches is not merely cognitive or intel-
lectual, it is existential, involving (when grasped) a dramatic per-
sonal transformation. The first stanza of Oliver's poem speaks
about this change in the language of rebirth: "Don't bother me. /
I've just / been born." These lines appear to anticipate the lesson
learned from the butterfly at the end. The poet's attention to "the
god of dirt" has led to spiritual rejuvenation, or, to use another
traditional word, "salvation." "Salvation" here means regaining a
sense of personal spiritual wholeness, integrity, and identity. It
means being in "a good place" in mind, body, and soul, and that
"place" is rooted in the earth. At the core of spiritual rejuvena-
tion is the sense of once again being at home in the world.

The "god of dirt" seems to be saying something similar to Jesus
when he warns of worrying too much about the future (Lk
12.22-31). The concern here is not about "forever"; it is anxiety
about having the basic necessities of life. "Look at the lilies," he
says. "They neither spin nor sew." They do not worry about the
future because God has provided for them. Humans should not
spend their lives striving after things, but strive for the "realm"
of God which is here and now (Mt 6.25-34).[5] I draw an analogy
between Jesus and Oliver because both are inviting us to look
and listen to *nature*. Birds and flowers, dogs, crows, frogs, and a
butterfly can teach us the deepest meaning of life.[6] In "Lilies" (*HL*
12; *NSP* 76) Oliver herself makes an explicit reference to the say-
ing of Jesus. She would like to live "like the lilies," but she rec-

ognizes that such living requires a dying, just as the lilies yield to the hungry tongues of cows. Readers familiar with the Bible cannot help but notice a similarity with the words of Jesus: "those who love their life lose it" (Jn 12.25; cf. Mt 10.39; Mk 8.35; Lk 17.33).

In fact, there are a number of biblical texts that present an analog to the voices that Oliver hears when she lies in the grass. The book of Proverbs often looks at subjects in nature for lessons about how to live, much as Jesus looked at lilies and ravens. The sages listen to the voices of leeches and fire, and they observe the behavior of ants, badgers, locusts, and lizards for wisdom (Prov 6.6–11; 30.15–16, 24–28). Sages can even garner a moral lesson by observing a dog returning to its vomit (Prov 26.11)! Job lectures to his contentious friends about the ways of God, advising them to "ask the animals, and they will teach you, the birds of the air, and they will tell you; ask the plants of the earth, . . . and the fish of the sea" (Job 12.7–8). Then there are other talkers like the infamous serpent of Genesis 3, a most articulate reptile, and the protesting donkey of Balaam, who can see an angel when the wizard is blind as a bat (Num 22.28). There are also mountains and hills that sing, accompanied by trees who clap their hands (Isa 55.12–13; Ps 148).

Psalm 19 merits even greater attention because it refers to *both* forms of "scripture": the Other Book of God (vv 1–6) and "the law of the Lord," i.e., decrees, ordinances, commandments, etc. (vv 7–13).[7] To pursue the question of nature's "voice," we shall look at the opening lines as an analog to Oliver's poem "One or Two Things," and then turn to her poem "The Sun." Psalm 19 begins:

> The heavens are telling the glory of God;
> and the firmament proclaims his handiwork.
> Day to day pours forth speech, and night to night
> declares knowledge.
> There is no speech, nor are there words; their voice
> is not heard;
> yet their voice goes out through all the earth,
> and their words to the end of the world.
> (vv 1–4a)

These opening verses contain no less than six words used synonymously with the word "tell": "proclaim," "speech," "declare," "words," "voice," and "utterance." The subjects of the verbs are the heavens, the firmament ("dome" in Gen 1.6), day and night.

The object of the verbs is God's glory, which, by virtue of synonymous parallelism is equated with God's "handiwork," i.e., the created world. In various ways the Psalm says that nature speaks of what poet Gerard Manley Hopkins called "the grandeur of God."[8] The speaking here is not necessarily to humans; perhaps it is better to say that we overhear this speaking, that we eavesdrop on nature's songs of praise. But, at the same time, the Psalm recognizes the ambiguity of this speech. In a seeming paradox, it says that "there is no speech," nor are there words, yet their voice and words permeate the entire world. How can nature speak and not speak at the same time?

The Psalm addresses the ambiguity inherent in all metaphors. A metaphor is a word or phrase that uses language inappropriate for a given subject to illuminate something about that subject that otherwise *cannot* be expressed. One of my favorite examples is the poem by Carl Sandburg in which he says that fog "comes on little cat feet."[9] Obviously, Sandburg does not mean this literally, that fog actually has cat paws. On the other hand, he *does* mean to say that sometimes there is a mysterious *presence* about fog that is like the silent slinking of a cat. Just as it would be foolish to take the metaphor literally (like the children's book character Amelia Bedelia), it would also be foolish to dismiss it as nonsensical. Those who have seen fog approaching and then engulfing them know that it has an uncanny vitality that a scientific description cannot approach ("dense water vapor in cloudlike masses close to the ground and limiting visibility").

Just as fog is and is not a cat, so nature speaks and yet does not speak. People do not hear words from trees and rocks and rivers the same way that they hear words spoken by other people. Yet there is a "voice," even if we have to put "voice" in quotation marks.[10] Children's books express the ambiguity most beautifully. In *The Other Way to Listen*, a young child learns from an old man how to hear the voices of nature. When the boy finally learns *how* to listen he hears the hills singing, but he says, "Of course their kind of singing isn't loud. It isn't any sound you can explain. It isn't made with words."[11] The Psalm, of course, goes a step further theologically. It says that the voice of nature reveals something about God, in this case, God's glory. Elsewhere, the heavens are said to tell of God's righteousness (Ps 50.6; 97.6). The heavens and mountains, forest and trees sing God's praise (Isa 44.23). Meadows and valleys "shout and sing together for joy" (Ps 65.13). As Joseph Sittler puts it, "God's creations in the world are his voice."[12] It may seem like self-congratulation when God's voice glorifies God, but here self-glorification is another expression for self-revelation.[13] The voices of creation function as God's envoys (to use one of Oliver's words), just as human prophets are envoys who glorify God (e.g., Isaiah 6; 40). As in the book of nature, so in the book of Scripture, we hear a voice that speaks and yet does not speak.[14] We should value what this voice tells us about God no less than we value what human voices tell us. As Terence Fretheim puts it, if the "natural metaphors for God are in some ways descriptive of God, then they reflect in their very existence, in their being what they are, the reality which is God."[15]

The analogy of hearing God's voice in the two Books of God presents a complex interpretive relationship that we cannot fully explore here. On the one hand, our reading of the contemporary poem is like our reading an *interpreter* of the Bible, rather than the Bible itself, because the poet is reading the book of nature and we are seeing that book through her eyes. On the other hand, when the poet asserts that "the god of dirt . . . said," it is comparable to the biblical *author* who asserts that "God said." As for the latter, most critical interpreters do not believe in a literal speaking by God; rather, they would agree with Dale Patrick when he writes, "at some point in the formation of the tradition, someone placed these words in [God's] mouth." For Patrick, the process involves "an intuitive sense" of the biblical author, who feels "addressed" by God.[16] That process, it seems to me, is exactly what we see in Oliver. When the biblical author and the contemporary poet report what God has said, they are both engaged in a "fictive" process of imagination.[17]

Psalm 19 offers us another perspective on nature's voice: It operates in cyclical time rather than historical time.

> In the heavens [God] has set a tent for the sun,
> which comes out like a bridegroom from his wed-
> ding canopy,
> and like a strong man runs its course with joy.
> Its rising is from the end of the heavens,
> and its circuit to the end of them;
> and nothing is hid from its heat. (vv 4c–6)

Here there is nothing new under the sun, to borrow a phrase from Ecclesiastes 1.9; indeed, it is the very *regularity* of the sun's circuit that reveals God's glory.[18] Already in verse 2 the Psalmist had pointed to the regularity of day and night as part of God's "handiwork." Elsewhere, this regularity is described as a "fixed order" (Jer 31.35–36; cf. 33.20). In fact, God ordained this order at the creation, providing "signs and seasons, days and years" (Gen 1.14). The reliability of nature's cycles thus presents a realm of divine involvement separate and distinct from that of historical events, where the prophets tell us that God is continually doing "a new thing" (Isa 43.19; 65.17). The circuit of the sun provides the fundamental necessity for all life—it heats the world and gives it light (v 6). The Hebrew slaves in Egypt needed the new thing of political revolution, but when they became Palestinian farmers, they welcomed the same old thing of nature's seasonal rhythms. We scoff at ancient people's unscientific fear that the sun would not come up in the morning, and their worshipping the sun as a god, but in Psalm 19 the author acknowledges something that we rarely think about—the sun is one of the most wonderful revelations of God's glory in nature. Oliver's poetry resembles that of the Psalmist when she says, "glory is my work" (LC 10).

What would it be like for us to appreciate the sun, not just after a week of dreary rain, or because we are heading to the beach, but simply because of its fundamental necessity for all of life? Oliver points the way in a poem called "The Sun" (NSP 50):

> Have you ever seen
> anything
> in your life
> more wonderful
>
> than the way the sun,
> every evening,
> relaxed and easy,
> floats toward the horizon
>
> and into the clouds or the hills,
> or the rumpled sea,
> and is gone—
> and how it slides again
>
> out of the blackness,
> every morning,
> on the other side of the world,
> like a red flower

streaming upward on its heavenly oils,
say, on a morning in early summer,
at its perfect imperial distance—
and have you ever felt for anything

such wild love—
do you think there is anywhere, in any language,
a word billowing enough
for the pleasure

that fills you,
as the sun
reaches out,
as it warms you

as you stand there,
empty-handed—
or have you too
turned from this world—

or have you too
gone crazy
for power,
for things?

We miss one of the most wonderful parts of life when we
turn away from this world, from one of the grandest displays of
nature. Why do we ignore such magnificence? Well, of course,
partly because the sun is there every day, no surprise. And we
know that it doesn't really come up and go down, but that its
"rising" and "falling" have to do with the earth's orbit. Our sci-
entific knowledge, of course, is an important part of our under-
standing of the world, but the resulting secularization has robbed
us of spiritual awe. As Abram says, "the sun and moon no
longer draw prayers from us but seem to arc blindly across the
sky."[19] But the poet is not interested in astronomy (as science);
the poet is interested in our continuing *perception* that the sun
appears to rise and set.[20] It is the very regularity (cyclical time)
that is part of the wonder, irrespective of the astronomical
method. Indeed, in her poem "Nature" Oliver says that in nature
"nothing new / / [will] ever happen, / which is the true gift of
nature, / which is the reason / we love it" (*HL* 55; *NSP* 90).[21]
But our inattention to the wonder of the sun has deeper causes

than our scientific knowledge. We have "gone crazy / for power, / for things." Materialism has eliminated naturalism. With another reference to Jesus, Oliver reverses the movement. She finds that to be "entirely poor" is to be "happy," and asks when did Jesus first sense such a direction ("Roses," WP 23). Her poem seems to echo Jesus' beatitude: "How happy are you who are poor" (Lk 6.20, Jerusalem Bible).

If we recall what we have learned about the Other Book of God, then we should be able to make the connection here between what Oliver helps us see in nature and what the Bible refers to as the "kingdom of God" (precisely what the poor will inherit). In fact, one of Oliver's poems describing an encounter with crows is entitled "Entering the Kingdom."[22] Opening ourselves to the wonder of the sun is also like entering a realm—in a sense that is implied by the reference to the sun as "imperial." Oliver's *seeing* the sun in a way that few of us do invites us to an exercise in "re-enchantment." Her *in-sight* encourages us to let down our sophisticated, scientific, rational understanding of the world and, in a sense, become "primitive" again. An exclusive investment in historical time prevents us from appreciating what one novelist calls "another, deeper layer of time, a time of stone and cloud and tree to which the time of clocks and calendars [is] a gross mockery cobbled up by savages."[23]

"Glory is my work," says the poet. "The heavens are telling the glory of God," says the Psalmist. Here juxtaposed are the two books of God. Moreover, the quotation from Scripture itself *refers* to the Other Book. Oliver hears the voice of nature that, in the biblical tradition, speaks of God. We would do well to listen with her ears.

TWO

Attitude

I N DISCUSSING HER APPROACH to writing, Oliver links spiritual-
ity, attention, and attitude:

> Now I think there is only one subject worth my
> attention and that is the recognition of the spiritual
> side of the world and, within this recognition,
> the condition of my own spiritual state. I am not
> talking about having faith necessarily, although
> one hopes to. What I mean by spirituality is not
> theology, but attitude. (WH 102).

The heart of natural spirituality is not what one thinks about
God, but how one relates to the natural world *as the realm of God.*
It is helpful to note that, in both Hebrew and Greek (the major
biblical languages), the word that we translate as "spirit" has the
primary meaning of "wind" or "breath." The spiritual is a deriv-
ative of the natural. Moreover, the divine breath animates all liv-
ing creatures, not just humans.[1] Our scientific knowledge of the
symbiosis of animal and plant life in the exchange of oxygen and
carbon dioxide only amplifies the interrelationship of all living
things. One author puts it this way: "The carbon dioxide we
exhale as a waste product becomes the life-giving force for a
plant; in turn, the oxygen waste of a plant gives us life. This
exchange of gas is what the word spirit means. Spirituality is
essentially the act of breathing."[2] Reflecting on the same phe-
nomenon in almost identical words, Abram suggests that the
air is "the soul of the visible landscape" and—in ancient
Mediterranean cultures—"a sacred presence."[3] Indeed, the inter-
dependence of animals (including us, of course) and plants
makes it "very difficult to discern, at any moment, precisely
where this living [human] body begins and where it ends."[4]
Similarly, in the biblical creation story of Genesis 2–3 the breath

that links us with all creatures has its counterpart in the earth (soil, ground) out of which all things animal, vegetable, and mineral are made—we are mud kin with "every tree" and "every animal of the field" (Genesis 2.7–9, 19). Together we make up a "dirty" family created by the God of dirt as a potter shapes clay.[5] This relationship belies the way we use the word "nature" to signify something *apart from* human beings, rather than the milieu that we are *part of.* The alienation between humans and the earth appears in the second half of the creation story in Genesis 2–3. Human alienation from the ground out of which we are made reflects a deeper alienation from the "Ground of our Being," to use one form of divine reference.[6]

Recognizing the "exchange of gas" and our mud kinship as the essence of our relationship to the world ought to be a rather humbling experience. The first order of a spiritual attitude toward the world is simply to *pay attention* to our place in it. As Augustine said, "Note it" (*attende*).

Oliver's poem "The Summer Day" (*HL* 60; *NSP* 94) will serve to introduce the religious dimensions to her attitude within nature.

> Who made the world?
> Who made the swan, and the black bear?
> Who made the grasshopper?
> This grasshopper, I mean—
> the one who has flung herself out of the grass,
> the one who is eating sugar out of my hand,
> who is moving her jaws back and forth instead of
>   up and down—
> who is gazing around with her enormous and
>   complicated eyes.
> Now she lifts her pale forearms and thoroughly washes
>   her face.
> Now she snaps her wings open, and floats away.
> I don't know exactly what a prayer is.
> I do know how to pay attention, how to fall down
> into the grass, how to kneel down in the grass,
> how to be idle and blessed, how to stroll through
>   the fields,
> which is what I have been doing all day.
> Tell me, what else should I have done?
> Doesn't everything die at last, and too soon?
> Tell me, what is it you plan to do
> with your one wild and precious life?

The poem begins with a theological question about creation: "Who made the world?" Quickly Oliver repeats and constricts the question in terms of specific animals—the swan, black bear, and grasshopper. Then she narrows her focus even more to attend only to the grasshopper. The cosmic question is reduced to a small insect in her hand, and almost half of the poem then looks at the grasshopper in great detail, as if the poet has become an entomologist full of wonder. She even notices the peculiar jaw movement of the grasshopper's eating. Here is an example of what John Muir called "grasshopper sermons."[7]

"To pay attention, this is our endless and proper work"—the first requirement of a spiritual attitude toward the world ("Yes! No!" WP 8).[8] This requirement may seem so obvious that it is needless to say, but, in fact, most of us do not pay attention to the natural world in our everyday lives. We are too busy, and very few of us work in a context that would bring us in contact with a grasshopper, much less a swan or a bear. Many children now spend far more time playing computer games (or soccer) than playing in the woods. Artist Georgia O'Keefe is famous for her paintings of flowers seen as if from a bee's eye view. But, as she has said, most people find it difficult to attend to the world around us because "really it takes time."[9] The failure to take time produces the incapability of experiencing an epiphany. The reverse appears in Oliver's allusion to the ancient Greek myth of an old couple who welcomes strangers, only to find that the strangers are gods who bless them: the couple "had almost nothing to give / / but their willingness / to be *attentive*" ("Mockingbirds," WP 16; cf. Genesis 18.1–14).[10]

In Oliver's poetry there is a deep appreciation for Sabbath time, the crown of creation in Genesis 1. Walter Brueggemann suggests the spiritual implications of the Sabbath: "keeping Sabbath, that is, breaking with the world of frantic self-securing, is a way to know God."[11] Oliver likes to "keep Sabbath," even if she does not use the term. In "The Summer Day," she says that she knows "how to be idle and blessed, how to stroll through the fields, / which is what I have been doing all day." Idleness—not work—produces blessing. There is an irony here, of course, in that Oliver's experience *becomes* work when she translates it into a poem, but she acknowledges the danger that "scribbling and crossing out" words can break her attention so that she almost misses what is before her ("The Notebook," HL 44).

Such an attitude toward time challenges a familiar proverb that says, "Idle hands are the Devil's workshop." Such a negative view of idleness prompts Oliver's rhetorical question, "Tell me, what else should I have done?" Elsewhere, the voice that would reject idleness is "ambition":

> Listen, says ambition, nervously shifting her weight from
> one boot to another—why don't you get going?
>
> For there I am, in the mossy shadows, under the trees.
>
> And to tell the truth I don't want to let go of the wrists
> of idleness, I don't want to sell my life for money,
> I don't even want to come in out of the rain.
> ("Black Oaks," WW 5).

Paying attention requires idleness, and far from being the Devil's workshop, this is sacred, Sabbath time.

The spiritual significance of paying attention also appears in Oliver's use of religious language, especially the word "prayer."[12] In "The Summer Day," she confesses that she does "not know exactly what a prayer is." But the next lines suggest that paying attention *is* a form of prayer, an association supported by the phrase "how to kneel down" (cf. LC 26). As Simone Weil has said, "Absolutely unmixed attention is prayer."[13] Of course, such prayer is not the usual talking to God. It is more like contemplation of what God has *made* (again, the opening lines). More particularly, the poet's attention is a special kind of listening and looking. The poet has ears that are sharply attuned to that elusive "voice" that Psalm 19 says is and yet is not there. The poet has eyes that can see what others cannot, a penetrating *in-sight* into the spiritual significance of the most ordinary things, such as a grasshopper. Moreover, prayer can be not only the poet's attention, but also what nature "says": "each pond with its blazing lilies / is a prayer heard and answered" ("Morning Poem," DW 6; NSP 106). Implicitly, here there is a conversation between pond and God whether or not humans can hear it.

In a sense, Oliver's insight is childlike in its simplicity and honesty, and especially in its sense of wonder. For Oliver, the command "Look!" is expressed in a way very much like a child who points to something that is all too familiar to us (breeding contempt, as the saying goes) but wondrously new to her. In fact, a phrase from one poem almost reads like a line from a children's primer: "look! look! look!"[14] In "First Snow" (AP 26; NSP 150) the silent "rhetoric" of the snow calls us to ask those basic, unanswerable questions that a child might ask: Why is there such beauty? How does it get here? Where does it come from? What does it mean? Oliver *senses* an answer, but does not think of one. In an autobiographical poem, "Aunt Leaf" (*TM* 47; *NSP* 196), Oliver remembers her childhood invention of the playful companion whom she called "Shining-Leaf, or Drifting-Cloud / or The-Beauty-of-the-Night." Aunt Leaf would "whisper in a language only the two of us knew," and they would travel on flights of fancy. Oliver's uncanny ability to continue this child-hood way of "pretending" as an adult is one of her greatest gifts as a poet. Nothing has been lost when we come to a poem like "The Swan" (*HL* 16; *NSP* 78) where "the path to heaven / / . . . [lies] in the imagination / with which you perceive / this world, / / and the gestures / with which you honor it."[15]

In a discursive essay Oliver has given us a description of her approach that echoes the language of Psalm 19:

> In the act of writing the poem, I am obedient, and submissive. Insofar as one can, I put aside ego and vanity, and even intention. *I listen.* What I hear is almost a voice, almost a language. It is a second ocean, rising, singing into one's ear, or deep inside the ears, whispering in the recesses where one is less oneself than a part of some single indivisible community.[16]

The auditory counterpart to the command to "look," there-fore, is the appeal to listen:

> *Listen, listen, I'm forever saying,*
>
> *Listen to the river, to the hawk, to the hoof,*
> *to the mockingbird, to the jack-in-the-pulpit—*
>
> then I come up with a few words, like a gift.
> ("Stars," *WW* 14).

To listen to the Other Book of God one must know another way to listen, one that includes not only a babbling brook or whistling bird but also the "voice" of plants like the jack-in-the-pulpit. Perhaps Oliver chooses that plant for its name, much as John Muir can talk about "plant people . . . preaching by the wayside."[17]

In her poems, what is "almost a voice, almost a language" appears in many forms. Moss can "lecture" even though it has "no tongues"; snow has a "white rhetoric"; trees emit an eloquent humming; creeks growl; rocks pant.[18] Oliver can hear the identical "sound, / not loud, / not unmusical" that mussels make when they are eating and when they are about to be taken *for* eating ("Mussels," *TM* 4; *NSP* 182). "There's no end to it, the kingdoms / crying out—and no end / / to the voices the heart can hear once / it's started" ("Winter Trees," *TM* 73). In short, all of these voices constitute "earth-talk" (*DW* 11).

For Oliver, the voices of nature (things animate *and* inanimate) are manifestations of a *communal* conversation. The most fundamental dimension of her attitude appears in her description of this peculiar language as a "whispering in the recesses where one is less oneself than a part of some single indivisible community" (*WH* 98).[19] Elsewhere she describes this community as a "family." In fact, in a poem called "The Family" she says, of "dark things [i.e., beasts] of the wood": "They are our brothers. / They are the family / We have run away from" (*NSP* 215). Her identity derives more from her participation in this family than from her individuality. Part of our problem is that "we are all / one family / / but we love ourselves / best" (*DW* 24). In order to overcome our "despair" of the world and our loneliness, we need to regain a sense of our "animal" nature, and so return to our "place / in the family of things" (*DW* 14; *NSP* 110).

Just as Oliver speaks of our "place in the family of things" and our rediscovery of this place as redemptive, so the "oral culture" instinctively "affirm[s] human kinship" with the world, recognizing that "mutual relations" must be maintained in order to preserve the health of the entire community.[20] Our very perception of the world is rooted in our "animal" nature, in ourselves as bodies, and our inseparable relationship with everything animate and inanimate. In fact, there really *is* no inanimate world. For Merleau-Ponty, the entire sensible world is "active, animate, and, in some curious manner, alive," and our perception of the world is inextricable from our *participation* in it—"a mutual interaction, an intercourse, 'a coition, so to speak, of my body with things.'"[21] Similarly, the presumed dichotomy between humans as subjects and everything else as objects disappears. Although that dichotomy is often identified with the scientific method, even much of contemporary science now rejects it as simplistic and, in fact, as a serious misconception of reality.[22] Instead, *all* phenomena are subjects and we live in a world of "intersubjectivity."[23]

In "Clapp's Pond," Oliver describes the moment when she is no longer simply an objective observer but a subjective participant:

> How sometimes everything
> closes up, a painted fan, landscapes and moments
> flowing together until the sense of distance—
> say, between Clapp's Pond and me—
> vanishes, edges slide together
> like the feathers of a wing, everything
> touches everything. (AP 21)

To say "the sense of distance . . . vanishes" is to say that the alienation between human and earth is momentarily suspended. In fact, Oliver says, "when I am doing my job well, I vanish" (BP 111). This dissolving of the ego bears a striking resemblance to the spiritual tradition of the *via negativa*, the spiritual path of self-negation. When I am "full of myself," I am not capable of entering into a relationship with another. When I "empty" myself, I am open to relationship—whether it is with a pond or another person or God. As the great mystic Meister Eckhart puts it, "God is not found in the soul by adding anything but by a process of subtraction."[24] Here we recall Oliver's self-description cited above, how she is "obedient and submissive," willing to "put aside ego and vanity." Oliver's capacity to "vanish" as subject and speak "on behalf of" other beings is nothing short of uncanny. She can, in effect, think like a whale, or a bear, or a minnow about to be devoured by an egret.[25]

When Oliver talks about animals and trees and rocks as the conversational family of which she is a part, she is not talking about mere personification. However childlike her attitude may be in some ways, she is definitely not interested in "cute" characters like Bambi or "Thumper" the rabbit or even a Charlotte the spider.[26] As she points out in a brief essay, portraying animals as cute prevents our understanding of nature as "a realm both sacred and intricate, as well as powerful, of which we are no more than a single part."[27] Her refusal to belittle any part of nature—animal, vegetable, or mineral—sounds like a renunciation of the "rule and conquer" anthropology implied in Genesis 1.28: "I would not be the overlord of a single blade of grass, that I might be its sister."[28] The more that we humanize nature, then, the more we express our alienation from it. Naming animals (Bambi), making them look and talk like us, robs them of their sacredness, that is, their holiness. To be holy means to be "set apart." Ironically, we cannot be a part of nature unless we can acknowledge its otherness. As Abram says of indigenous cultures, our "otherness" as humans is made "eerily potent" precisely by our "familial" connection.[29] For Oliver, the goal is not to make animals human, but, by imaginative attention, to intuit what it might be like to be an animal. It is the very wildness of animals that makes them spiritually significant. Domestication—whether physical or metaphorical—robs them of their otherness and reduces them to playthings.[30]

Such domestication appears in one of Oliver's poems dealing explicitly with religious tradition—"Christmas Poem" (TM 64). In the beginning, Oliver invokes the legend of the barnyard animals who go "down on their knees" at midnight on Christmas Eve, in honor of the birth of Christ. But when Oliver goes to the barn, she discovers only beasts who "lay in their stalls like stone. / / Oh the heretics!" Yet in simply being themselves, the animals testify to the timeless "Now!" instead of the events of "history." Rather than the characters of legend, they are the "citizens of the pure, the physical world, / . . . powerful / of body, peaceful of mind." It is precisely in their being as animals that they are "no heretics, but a miracle, / immaculate still as when you thundered forth / on the morning of creation!"[31] To paraphrase a book title on biblical ecology, they are miraculous in being "natural, not supernatural."[32] Then, in the concluding stanza, Oliver is "listening again" to the story of Jesus' birth, but the barnyard animals are comforting her, as if she were a child. The legend clothes the animals in human characteristics; in the poem, the animals cuddle the poet with their earthy warm bodies.[33]

When Oliver speaks of nature as "family" she is talking seriously about a personal *relationship*, indeed, a *spiritual* relationship. In "Some Questions You Might Ask," Oliver wonders "Who has [a soul], and who doesn't?" (HL 1; NSP 65) The poem remains interrogative, but clearly Oliver wishes to include all the "family" as soulful. "Why should I have it, and not the camel?" Or, she adds, maple trees, stones, roses, grass, lemons. In her essays she explains that she does not talk "about" these things, but "on their behalf," because everything from a thunderstorm to a daffodil is "a company of spirits, as well as bodies" (WH 102). Everything from cats to fence posts to chairs "is alive" and "are all animate, and have spirits" (WH 99; cf. BP 63; LC 30).

Some pious readers may balk at this point, once again judging the allocation of "spirit" or "soul" to ordinary things as a kind of pagan animism. Isn't this what our "developed" religions left behind? Yes, say some philosophers of language, and it was a sad day of departure. Precisely *because* of our inextricable participation in the world, Abram himself can even say, "we are *all* animists."[34] Moreover, as we have seen, biblical traditions reflect the view that at least all *animate* things have spirit because *their* spirits also derive from the divine breath (e.g., Psalm 103.27-30). Even if Scripture did not offer support for appreciating the spirits of non-human things, if our subject is the book of *nature* as the Other Book of God, as I have argued, then we are looking to poets like Oliver to help us read that *other* book. What she sees is an independent *supplement* to biblical scripture, with its own integrity. Moreover, as Rosemary Ruether has pointed out, animism "does not mean deification of nature, but simply the recognition of personlike life in nature. The denial of this is distinctly peculiar to the modern West."[35] Indeed, she asserts that for early Christians "Even animals and plants had soul, and the human soul shared with them the animal and vegetative soul."[36]

Just as there is nothing "cute" about the inhabitants of Oliver's world, so there is no room for sentimentality. In particular, there is no tolerance for seeing only the beauty of nature. In fact, one cannot fully appreciate the beauty unless one also acknowledges the brutality or even the "terror."[37] "All my life," says Oliver, "and it has not come to any more than this: beauty and terror" (*BP* 48). The doomed minnow of "The Egret" is a case in point (*NSP* 47). The poem describes what the death of a minnow would look like from the point of view of the minnow. The minnow makes a single, fatal error, mistaking the egret's bamboo legs for reeds. Then the "white flame" of the egret's head lunges and the minnow is no more. "They were here, / they were silent, / they are gone, having tasted / sheer terror." To a certain degree, these lines about a minnow reflect what life is like for all creatures, including humans. Life is incredibly fragile and transitory, subject to instant and unexpected death. "Look! Look!" says Oliver. Look at the inseparable combination of beauty and brutality all wrapped up in an egret. We cannot really see the egret's beauty unless we *look* at how it kills to survive. Elsewhere that bird provides a comforting vision of "white fire" in a "black and empty" world, "stepp[ing] / over every dark thing" ("Egrets," *AP* 19; *NSP* 148); here the "white flame" brings "dark death." So the poem ends with the poet's "invented words"—translating for us that elusive "voice" of nature: "What is this dark death / that opens / like a white door?"

The egret and the minnow are one among numerous examples of the principle that the necessity for food (among carnivores) leads to suffering for animals, and Oliver cites Teilhard de Chardin's comment that this necessity is "man's most agonizing spiritual dilemma" (WH 19). So crows dream of revenge on the owl, who brings the "unalterable fact" of death ("In the Pinewoods, Crows and Owl," AP 9). So Oliver is "nourished / by the mystery" involved with her catching and eating a fish. Indeed, her eating the fish is part of what joins them together ("I am the fish, the fish / glitters in me" ["The Fish," AP 56; NSP 165]). Similarly, although Oliver can empathize with a hibernating bear to the extent that they share "The family name," within two pages she can also identify with the hunter who eats a bear who (like the fish) "will come to live inside me" and whose meat brings her in touch with "the dense orb that is all of us."[38] In sum, "The terror of the country / Is prey and hawk together" ("Winter in the Country," NSP 214; cf. "The Rabbit," NSP 221). If our attitude toward the world is to be realistic, we must see "the beauty / of the blue shark cruising toward the tumbling seals" ("Cold Poem," AP 31). As far as wild animals are concerned, carnivores dominate the "company of spirits."[39]

But brutality is not limited to the necessity for food. It extends to virtually every form of "terror" that one could imagine: kidnapped children, parental sexual abuse, the Holocaust, a stillborn kitten with only one eye, the slaughter of buffalo (not to mention Native Americans), and sailors who will not talk about the beauty of the sea because they live in fear of its waves.

The "dark side" is prominent on two of the occasions when Oliver refers explicitly to God (or gods). In "The Shark" (DW 69), Oliver describes the catching and grisly mutilation of a shark as a kind of exposé of human cruelty against an animal that "had no speech to rail against this matter." She then says that "we will all cry out last words," but "Whoever He is, count on it: He won't answer." In fact, God ("the inventor") is as callous as the shark's "hunter," for whom the shark's agony is "remote, unfelt." Similarly, in a poem about a friend's death from cancer, Oliver says, "there are no gods" to save her ("For Eleanor," TM 58).

The apathetic God of "The Shark" is too busy off creating other worlds to attend to the suffering of the shark, much less rescue it from death. Is this God identical to the "god of dirt"? We might think not. We might see here a rejection of a ruthless

"patriarchal" deity, or, worse, of "theological sadism."[40] Yet the
God of this poem is no *less* responsive or interventionist in
preventing the suffering of the shark as God presumably is with
regard to the brutality involved in the death of many other crea-
tures in Oliver's poems. One might argue that the *human* brutal-
ity here is merely for sport, not for food, distinguishing the act
of killing from that of (other) animals. But the terror of the
shark's death is no less than that of the minnows that we
watched being devoured by the egret, or rabbits caught in the
claws of the owl, or a teal chick mangled and swallowed by a
snapping turtle (*HL* 22). After all, the terror of "The Shark" is the
inverse of what we have already seen: "the beauty / of the blue
shark cruising toward the tumbling seals" (*AP* 31), and sharks
always pose a threat to humans in return ("Sharks," *TM* 33).

Anyone who at first is offended by comparing God to a cruel
hunter, or proclaiming the failure (or refusal, inability?) of God
to cure disease, need only pause for a moment to recognize how
utterly true to human experience Oliver's poems are. Within
Judeo-Christian tradition it is certainly possible to entertain an
image of God who, at times, at least *seems* to be malevolent.
Beginning with the Bible, but continuing down to the latest
tragedy, people have raged against the apparent absence or even
cruelty of God in the face of pain, suffering, and death. The
Psalmists of the Hebrew Bible often complain of God's absence,
and Job even accuses God of slashing open his kidneys (Job
16.13)! As one scholar suggests, the God of Job shows that "the
forces that can destroy us are restrained by nothing more than
a horsehair, and this resides in the hands of a God who often
seems cruelly capricious."[41] Even Jesus quoted the Psalms in his
despairing cry from the cross: "My God, my God, why have you
forsaken me?" And Jesus receives no answer this side of death.
In fact, one can at least infer some allusions to crucifixion in
"The Shark." The phrase "we will all cry out last words" may
remind us of the "last words" of Christ. Similarly, the mutilated,
dead shark is "winched into the air; men / lifting the last bloody
hammers."[42]

Contemporary writers like C. S. Lewis have raged against the
apparent cruelty of God as a "Cosmic Sadist."[43] Even though one
(like Lewis) may not end up with such a theology, sometimes
such railing is simply a healthy recognition of the brutality of
life as it is. A book on prayer talks about aggression and anger
in prayer this way:

> We feel speechless fury at the irreversible events in
> life, events that seem senseless, cruel, and cause
> deep suffering, events that arouse our deepest fear
> and anger. Death stuns us still in the loss of a
> dearly loved person, the painful illness of a child,
> the sudden accident that wipes out a life or maims
> it . . . Aggression helps us hold on in the imageless
> dark when we hear no answer and feel no result.[44]

In other words, raging at God is a way of venting such aggres-
sion, even if the accompanying *image* of God (as the causative
agent) is not really rational, or not what one would otherwise
hold. The response is as much emotional as intellectual. On the
other hand, one of Oliver's poems would serve as a healthy cor-
rective to that simplistic theology that sees tragic accidents and
natural disasters as the work of God. In "Shadows" (DW 17),
Oliver acknowledges the "grief" caused by "Cyclone, fire, and
their merry cousins," producing "bodies in the river, / or bones
broken by the wind." But, she says, "the waters [of the flood]
rise without any plot." In other words, one should not look for
and cannot find any intention or purpose behind such tragedies:
"whatever / the name of the catastrophe, it is never / the oppo-
site of love."[45]

In short, fundamental to Oliver's attitude toward nature is the
acknowledgement of this truth: "nothing's important / / except
that the great and cruel mystery of the world . . . / not be
denied" ("The Turtle," HL 22, referring to the turtle's eating of
the teal chick, mentioned above). Nevertheless, sometimes the
dark is also the way to the light, involving a mythic theme of
death and resurrection. The theme is apparent in the title of one
poem: "The Lilies Break Open Over the Dark Water" (HL 40;
NSP 88). Just so, the poppy "shines like a miracle" despite "the
indigos of darkness" ("Poppies," NSP 39). Because of their "faith
in the world," egrets can step "over every dark thing" ("Egrets,"
AP 19; NSP 148). A dead black snake in the road betrays the mer-
ciless suddenness of death, but also "the light at the center of
every cell" that animated the snake in life ("The Black Snake,"
TM 9; NSP 184).

There is often a *movement* from dark to light. Death (which
Oliver calls *Oblivion and Co.*)[46] is always followed in some way
by new life. For Oliver, the first principle of earth's economy—
all waste becomes food—is essentially nature's version of resur-
rection. So we both honor and loathe vultures, who "minister"

to the earth by performing "the miracle: / resurrection" ("Vultures," AP 37; NSP 155). The "Moccasin Flowers" stand "shining / and willing" before falling to "oblivion," yet in the end they "become the trees" (HL 2; NSP 66). Oliver buries a dead rabbit, after waiting days for it "miraculously to heal / and spring up / joyful," but after the burial she finds a bird's nest with chicks warmed by the rabbit's fur and she asks, mockingly, "are you listening, death?" ("The Rabbit," NSP 221).

What Oliver calls "resurrection" here we might more accurately characterize as "reincarnation," admitting, however, that neither term will conform to orthodox religious doctrines. At least, resurrection here does not seem to refer to personal, human continuity after death. In fact, in one poem Oliver diverts the topic of a "personal heaven" where we will rejoin others to that perpetuity exhibited by the natural world of foxes and roses. If she had "another life," that is what she would choose to be, because foxes and roses live their lives in "unstinting happiness" rather than asking the "foolish [and fearful] question" of what will become of them after death ("Roses, Late Summer," HL 66; NSP 95). "Resurrection," therefore, seems to refer to a return to that larger "family" to which all beings belong.[47] That return is part of the process that produces or nurtures new life in some form—the ecological benefits of brutality. Owls—some of the most frequent predators in Oliver's poems—"are what keeps everything / enough, but not too many" ("Bowing to the Empress," DW 55). In fact, one of the poems that describes the owl's bloody feeding is called "Praise" (HL 46).[48]

Again, Oliver's view of death as the great "recycler" resembles the view of oral peoples. As Abram suggests, for Hopi peoples, "in the eternal cycle, death feeds life."[49] Death is not escape from the material world into an immaterial heaven; rather, death is "a transformation in the land." "In an old Pawnee tale, a dead man returns as a ghost, saying 'I am in everything; in the grass, the water.'"[50] Just so, Oliver speculates that maybe we will rise not as angels but "as grass" ("Gravel," LC 44). Despite its apparent unorthodoxy, Oliver's naturalistic view of "life after death" also resembles that of at least some theologians for whom ecology is central. Ruether, for example, concludes from our scientific knowledge of the world that there is no "heaven" separate from the world to which we go after death.[51] In fact, death is "the means by which all living things are returned to earth to be regenerated as new organisms."[52] Oliver's poems on brutality and beauty, death and regeneration, thus fit with those theologians for whom ecocentrism (ecology) has replaced anthropocentrism (anthropology). Nothing less than our worldview is at stake. As Daniel Cowdin suggests, the processes of nature described by ecological theologians as normative (even desirable) are denounced by long-standing tradition as in need of redemption: cyclical time, predation and competition, suffering and death.[53] For such theologians (as, I think, for Oliver) there will be no world where the "wolf shall live with the lamb" (Isa 12:6), or, to use one of Oliver's metaphors, where the sharks will play with the tumbling seals rather than eat them.

In Oliver's poetry, death loses none of its sting or its mystery. However natural the process, it causes us pain and grief. So Oliver laments the death of a favorite oak tree and its gradual dissolution into the earth (thanks to the feeding of yeasts that gnaw on it like wolves). It was the *living* tree that she loved ("The Oak Tree," *HL* 52). Yet we have seen that the movement in nature's cycles can reveal that "death is an imposter" ("Gannets," *NSP* 28). Moreover, this movement from death to resurrection also applies to human spiritual transformation. The poem "Skunk Cabbage" is exemplary (*AP* 44; *NSP* 160). The poem is about spring, when the ice on the ponds begins to break up, and someone is "dreaming of ferns and flowers." Instead she comes upon a skunk cabbage emerging "through the chilly mud." She kneels beside it. Its smell is "lurid" and its leaves hold the carcasses of dead insects. It is an "appalling" plant with its "thick root nested below." "But," says Oliver, "these are the woods you love, / where the secret name / of every death is life again." It is not delicate "ferns, leaves, [and] flowers" that start the process, but the rough "brawn" of the skunk cabbage that "pull[s] down the frozen waterfall, the past." And then comes the concluding line: "What blazes the trail is not necessarily pretty." The way to new life is a "stubborn / and powerful," ugly and smelly journey "through the chilly mud."[54]

The personal transformation intimated in "Skunk Cabbage" is explicit in "Crossing the Swamp" (*AP* 58; *NSP* 166), using similar imagery. The swamp is the "wet thick / cosmos, the center / of everything," "peerless mud." The mud represents how difficult it is for us "trying / for a foothold, fingerhold, / mindhold." Here Oliver's imagery is virtually an exact equivalent of those biblical Psalms of lament in which the psalmist cries out of "the desolate Pit, the miry bog," in which "there is no foothold" (Psalms 40.2; 69.2). Yet in the end the poet is immersed in "earth-soup," and finds herself strangely nurtured and revived by these

           succulent marrows
               of earth—a poor
    dry stick given
        one more chance
    . . . .
    [to] take root,
        sprout, branch out, bud—

Only after looking at both the darkness and the light in
Oliver's poems can we adequately appreciate a final aspect of her
attitude: amazement. In a sense, amazement is an extension of
the childlike wonder to which I referred earlier, but, to use Paul
Ricoeur's well-known phrase, amazement is a *second naiveté*."[55]
When Oliver pays attention, when she takes the time to listen
and look, claiming her place in "the family of things," seeing both
the dark and the light, she is amazed. In fact, it is striking how
often her use of the word appears precisely in a poem about
death and decay. In "The Ponds," when she "bend[s] closer" and
looks carefully at the lilies she discovers that, in fact, they are
not as perfect as they appear from a distance, that they are "lop-
sided," "blight[ed]," and "nibbled away," "full of unstoppable
decay." "Still," she says, "what I want in my life / is to be will-
ing / to be dazzled," "to believe that the imperfections are noth-
ing— / . . . And I do" (HL 58; NSP 92). In one of her most vivid
poems about death, "White Owl Flies Into and Out of the Field"
(HL 79; NSP 99), Oliver wonders if *our* death is not like that of
an animal caught and killed by a white owl: "maybe death / isn't
darkness, after all, / but so much light / wrapping itself around
us" (cf. the minnow and the egret, discussed above). Only then
will we be "weary / of looking, and looking"—remember "Look!
Look! Look!"—"and shut our eyes, / not without amazement."
Finally, in what almost amounts to an autobiographical epitaph
("When Death Comes," NSP 10), she says,

    When it's over, I want to say: all my life
    I was a bride married to amazement.
    I was the bridegroom, taking the world into my arms.

Included in the meaning of "amazement" is admiration.
Oliver's poems exhibit, I think, much what the character Shug
says in what we might call the "title passage" of Alice Walker's
The Color Purple (and it is a "colorful" passage indeed!): "'More

than anything else, God love admiration . . . just wanting to share a good thing. I think it pisses God off if you walk by the color purple in a field somewhere and don't notice it."[56] Admiration is where attention leads, if one is truly looking and listening. Admiration and astonishment are or should be part of our gratitude for the world ("Gratitude," WK 40). In fact, Oliver does call her work "praise poems" (WH 102), and, as we have noted before, in her most recent work Oliver's admiration seems to become more explicitly theological, if not even confessional.[57] She can issue what appears to be a call to worship: "Adore him" (LC 50).

As we shall see more fully below, the woods are her "temple." There "Under the trees, along the pale slopes of sand, I walk in an ascendant relationship to rapture, and with words I celebrate this rapture, I see, and dote upon, the manifest."[58] Of course, what she means by "rapture" is far different from the popular meaning (i.e., the ascent of the faithful into heaven at the last judgment). To invoke the title of a recent popular book series, Oliver would rather be among those "left behind" rather than those transported to heaven. Nevertheless, "rapture" has a long association with traditionally religious experience. Along with amazement, it is associated especially with awe and wonder. As theologian Abraham Heschel has written, "Wonder or radical amazement is the chief characteristic of the religious man's attitude toward history and nature." "*The beginning of awe is wonder, and the beginning of wisdom is awe.*"[59] In a kind of confirmation of Oliver's own use of the word "attitude," Heschel defines awe further: "Awe is a sense for the transcendence, for the reference everywhere to Him who is beyond all things. It is an *insight* better conveyed in *attitudes* than in words."[60] That is, such insight cannot be defined so much as witnessed in operation, which, I think, is precisely what we see when we look at the world through Oliver's eyes. In the end, the theologian and the poet have much in common: "What I mean by spirituality is not theology, but attitude" (WH 102).

THREE

Flora *and* Fauna

1. The Blessing Tree

> Only the half brother understood the atavistic
> yearning that swept him when he stood beneath
> the trees, when a branch in the wind made the
> sound of an oboe. He had only to walk into the
> woods far enough to lose the camp, and he was in
> an ancient time that lured him but which he could
> not understand in any way. . . . He could hear a
> little drum, a chant. But what could it mean? The
> kernel of life, tiny, heavy, deep red in color, was
> secreted in these gabbling woods. How could he
> understand it? (E. Annie Proulx, *Postcards*, 165)

AMONG THE NUMEROUS medieval references to the Other
Book of God, that of St. Bernard resonates with the "gab-
bling woods" of Proulx's novel, although Bernard seems
to find the woods more articulate: "Believe me who have tried.
Thou wilt find something more in woods than in books. Trees
and rocks will teach thee what thou canst not hear from a mas-
ter."[1] In the book of Scripture, however, you will not find any
such appreciation for the spiritual communication of trees. They
may provide part of the setting of a story (1 Kgs 19.4; Lk 19.4),
or provide a metaphor or symbol (Ezek 31.1-18; Mt 13.32), or may
even be included in a hymn of praise for God's creation (Ps
104.16f). In fact, trees are occasionally ascribed voices (or hands)
to join in that praise, along with other parts of creation (Ps 148.8;
Isa 44.23; 55.12).[2] Nevertheless, virtually nowhere do trees, *simply
as trees*, enjoy the focus of the author's attention.[3]

If there is an exception it appears in the "tree of life." A wide-
spread symbol of rejuvenation and eternal life, in the Hebrew
Bible this tree is a simile for wisdom, sometimes personified.[4] Of

course, post-biblical Christian tradition has also portrayed the cross as the tree of life, a version of the central Christian symbolism of death and resurrection. However, this Christian "conversion," as it were, again illustrates the tendency to see the significance of trees in terms of historical events, rather than in trees simply as trees. The so-called "legend of the dogwood" is a popular example of this conversion. The gnarled trunk and rust-like coloring on the edge of the white flowers, as well as the "crown" in the middle, are ascribed to the notion that it was the dogwood from which the cross was made. Formerly a tall, stately tree, the dogwood became deformed because it was used for the crucifixion of Jesus, its flowers marked by the "stains" of Jesus' wounds and displaying his crown of thorns. Yet the loveliness of the white petals proclaims the resurrection. In short, both the ostensible "ugliness" of the tree and its beauty are reduced to historical causes.[5] A similar conversion happened to the Christmas tree. No longer was it a "pagan" symbol of eternal life simply because it is an *evergreen*, but because it is associated with the birth of Christ.

My purpose here is not to be the Grinch who stole Christmas (or Easter). Rather, it is to illustrate with reference to a single natural subject—a tree—why we need to turn to the Other Book of God if we are to appreciate the *natural spiritual* significance of trees. On the one hand, the conversion of dogwood and evergreen, as well as eggs and even the *name* "Easter," to Christian symbols was part of the process of syncretism that is rooted in the Bible itself.[6] Native American–Catholic syncretism illustrates the same process when a corn dance is associated (however loosely) with a patron saint. Here nature is at least incorporated into the central symbol system of the faith. On the other hand, there is a price to be paid, and that price is the implication or even dogma that the *real* significance of a natural subject is its "historical nature," not, to employ an awkward yet telling phrase, its natural nature.

How then shall we approach a tree as a subject with its own spiritual significance, rather than simply an associative significance? A classic passage from Martin Buber's *I and Thou*[7] will help to lead us into a poem by Oliver. "I consider a tree," says Buber. As in all of our experience, there are two forms that such consideration can take. I can consider the tree as an object, an "It." Or I can consider it as a subject, a "Thou." The two are not mutually exclusive. I do not have to give up my "objective" understanding of the tree—say, my scientific knowledge of photosynthesis or forest ecology—in order to enter into a "subjective" experience with the tree. Nevertheless, the subjective consideration is profoundly different. "Subjective" here does not mean simply internal, with reference to me. It has to do instead with the *tree* as *subject* rather than object. To use Buber's key word, when I consider the tree as subject I stand "in relation" to it. Buber's emphasis on our interrelationship with the world reminds us of its "intersubjectivity." As Abram says, "that tree bending in the wind" is an intersubjective phenomenon—"experienced by a multiplicity of sensing subjects"—more real than the supposed reality of objectivism.[8]

Buber insists that this relationship between me and the tree is not merely an "impression" that I have, or a "play of my imagination" (our phrase would be a "figment of my imagination"). Rather, the tree "is bodied over against me and has to do with me, as I with it—only in a different way." In other words, there is something really *there* in the tree that relates to me. The relationship really is two-way, and the tree as subject is not simply something that I *impose* on the tree. "Relation is mutual." That the tree is "bodied" with respect to me suggests that we are not simply minds but "body subjects," and it is through the body that we relate most profoundly to the world.[9] Abram's way of putting it echoes Buber's: "In the act of perception . . . I enter into a sympathetic relation with the perceived. . . . From within the depths of this encounter, we know the thing or phenomenon only as our interlocutor—as a dynamic presence that confronts us and draws us into relation."[10]

But does the tree, then, have "consciousness"? Of this, says Buber, we "have no experience." Yet, having entered into a relationship with the tree ourselves, we should not dismiss the relational integrity of the tree out of hand. "I encounter no soul or dryad of the tree," Buber concludes, "but the tree itself." By the latter statement, Buber appears to mean that we also cannot dismiss the subjective reality of the tree by saying that it is another reality *inhabiting* it, in particular a "dryad," which means some form of divine being such as a nymph. No, it is "the tree itself" that relates to me. Similarly, Abram suggests that "the [primitive] world [is] made up of multiple intelligences," and we should not dismiss these intelligences as either "supernatural" or "internal" (i.e., "all in our head," as we say).[11]

Buber's thought apparently changed over time. An original view of the human/nature relationship as one of fusion ("you feel the bark as your skin") became one in which the distinctiveness

•:•

29

of both human and tree was maintained. The tree remains "other" than me even as I relate to it, in such a way that the relationship does not rob the tree of its own integrity.[12] Oliver, as we have seen, is capable of the same distinction, especially with animals. However much she may "get into their skin," as it were, they are "other" at the same time as being our "family."

In the passage immediately previous to the tree consideration (p. 6), Buber suggests that there are, in fact, three "spheres" of our relationships: with nature, other people, and "spiritual beings." Only in human relationships does speech really take place. Yet it would seem that both human relationships and relationships with nature are also "spiritual" to the extent that in *all* relationships we meet "the eternal *Thou*": "in each we are aware of a breath from the eternal *Thou*; in each *Thou* we address the eternal *Thou*." Not surprisingly, given Buber's blend of Jewish philosophical mysticism, his appreciation for the divine "breath" reminds us of the biblical taxonomy in which all creatures are so "inspired." Reflecting on the same mystical tradition, Abram puts it this way: "Like the wind itself, the breath of God permeates all of nature."[13]

With the background of Buber's *I and Thou*, we may now turn to Oliver again. We begin with prose from her recent collection of essays, *Winter Hours*:

> I am one of those who has no trouble imagining
> the sentient lives of trees, of their leaves in some
> fashion communicating or of the massy trunks and
> heavy branches knowing it is I who have come, as
> I always come, each morning, to walk beneath
> them, glad to be alive and glad to be there.
> (WH 15)

> Eventually I began to appreciate—I don't say this
> lightly—that the great black oaks knew me. I don't
> mean they knew me as myself and not another—
> that kind of individualism was not in the air—but
> that they recognized and responded to my pres-
> ence, and to my mood. They began to offer, or I
> began to feel them offer, their serene greeting.
> (WH 96)

Here, it seems to me, Oliver offers a poet's experience of the type of relationship described in Buber's classic terms. Her feeling of being recognized and greeted by trees is a natural expansion of the rich sense in which Buber understood "meeting" and "mutuality."

Now in "A Blessing" (TM 75) Oliver attends to one specific tree:

> The man in the tree, a rough amorphous pope
> Making the sign of benediction over
>
> The pasture, and my daily walk,
> Has stood for years
>
> Locked in the wrinkled bark halfway up
> The black oak tree.
>
> I have had in my lifetime many
> Blessings, from father, mother, friends,
>
> From dogs and strangers. But none
> Washed like the water
>
> Of these green arms lifted
> To a distant heaven, yet including me.
>
> How shall I walk in the world,
> But looking for light and wisdom,
>
> Believing in what I see,
> And more—what turns
>
> On the wheel of what cannot be defined
> In the leaves, in the darkness?

The poem reminds us of the hallmarks of Oliver's attitude toward "the world." She attends to it, "looking for light and wisdom, / / Believing in what I see." What she sees "cannot be defined" in a discursive sense, just as the shape in the tree is "amorphous," yet the reality of the *presence* of the tree is unquestionable. They *respond* to each other.

The religious language in this poem is obvious. Like the man in the moon, there is a man in the tree, a priest, indeed, a pope. His arms (presumably limbs of the tree) are raised to heaven, a traditional priestly gesture, and he is making "the sign of benediction" that embraces the poet in her walk. The benediction imparts blessing, one that surpasses all others received by family, friends, "dogs and strangers." The excellence of the blessing lies in its baptismal power: it "washed like the water" over her (rain falling from the leaves?). If the allusion is, in fact, to baptism, as it appears, then this poem is about spiritual cleansing and rejuvenation, or even death and new life. At least those are the symbolic associations that baptism would imply.[14]

The blessing bestowed by nature is central to another poem, "The Fawn" (TM 13):

> Sunday morning and mellow as precious metal
> the church bells rang, but I went
> to the woods instead.
>
> A fawn, too new
> for fear, rose from the grass
> and stood with its spots blazing,
> and knowing no way but words,
> no trick but music,
> I sang to him.
>
> He listened.
> His small hooves struck the grass.
> Oh what is holiness?
>
> The fawn came closer,
> walked to my hands, to my knees.
>
> I did not touch him.
> I only sang, and when the doe came back
> calling out to him dolefully
> and he turned and followed her into the trees,
> still I sang,
> not knowing how to end such a joyful text,
>
> until far off the bells once more tipped and tumbled
>   and rang through the morning, announcing
> the going forth of the blessed.

This is a Sabbath poem. It is Sunday morning, and the poet goes to "the church in the wildwood" (to borrow from an old hymn), only for Oliver the church is the wildwood. As she says in one of her essays, "For me the door to the woods is the door to the temple" (WH 98).

Immediately a fawn rises out of the grass with "its spots blazing." The poet, being human, has no way to communicate with the fawn except to use words, and to sing. So, she sings, and the fawn listens. Here is the "soul at attention," both the soul of the poet and the soul of the fawn. Indeed, the fawn not only listens, he *responds* to her song by striking his hooves against the grass. This momentary relationship between poet and animal introduces the central line of the poem: "Oh what is holiness?"[15]

The answer implicit in the poem and in all of Oliver's work is that this *moment* is holy. This place and time are sacred, because here is what Buber calls a *meeting* of human and animal, an instance of communion that bridges the alienation between them. "The fawn came closer, / walked to my hands, to my knees." It is as if the childlike "second naiveté" of the poet and the ingenuousness of the fawn ("too new / for fear") combine to produce an epiphany. Holiness is not something limited to the religious world, much less the supernatural; holiness is something that happens *in* the natural world. As Oliver says of another such encounter, this is "the world / that is ours, or could be," if we would only attend to it, and such attention is "how you pray" ("Five A.M. in the Pinewoods," *HL* 32; *NSP* 83). Although Oliver does not make an explicit theological move, we should not hesitate to say that holiness here, between fawn and poet, includes a revelation of the divine. In a word, something of God is present in this moment. To use Buber's language again, in the relationship between poet and fawn, they also meet the "eternal Thou." The sacredness of space and time here is identical to one author's description of Navajo sensibility: "That which is within and that which surrounds one is all the same and it is holy."[16]

Even when the fawn is called away by the doe, Oliver sings on because she is filled with joy. Combined with the first stanza, the closing stanza forms a frame, returning to Sabbath and the (traditional) churchgoers. The renewed ringing of the bells brings an end to the service and to the poet's joy, just as the initial ringing marked the beginning of the service and her entry into the woodland sanctuary. The bells announce "the going forth of the blessed," but implicitly the blessing includes *both* kinds of churchgoers, those who leave the building and the poet who leaves the woods.

The title of the poem about the tree—"A Blessing"—serves as an umbrella for "The Fawn" and many other poems by Oliver.

Here we see in the book of nature what a theologian calls the "blessing presence" of God, even though Oliver's poem is not overtly theistic.[17] Blessing is the potent vitality that is present in all things, identified by various religious traditions in different ways.

Fred Chappell gives a vivid description of blessing in one of his novels. A sociologist who is studying Appalachian culture has gone to a square dance. As he watches the dance, he suddenly ceases to be the objective analyst and, instead, is caught up in the fervor. He realizes that he is "linked" not only with the people there, but also "with nonhuman nature, with sky and stream and mountain, in its *reverences*." He feels close to "a *strength* that helped to *animate* the world, a *power* that joined all things together in a pattern that lay just barely beyond the edge of comprehension." Even this power, felt in the dance, is "but a streamlet of the larger current that poured through the world and everything that was in the world and beyond it."[18] The sociologist and the poet are attuned to the same reality, what Oliver calls "a power that is not you but flows / into you like a river" (TM 27; NSP 191).

2. "The Calving of the Deer"

> "Do you know when the mountain goats
> give birth?
> Do you observe the calving of the deer?"
> (Job 39.1)

In the biblical book that bears his name, Job is an innocent man who has lost virtually everything—his possessions, his children, and his health. Job demands an explanation from God, but God remains silent until near the end, when God speaks "out of the whirlwind" (chapters 38–41). But what God says is far from what Job wants. Job wants to know how God can be just if an innocent person suffers. Instead God asks him what *he* knows about all sorts of wild creatures—lions and ravens, mountain goats and deer, the wild ass and ox, the ostrich, the hawk, and the vulture. Instead of a courtroom, Job gets a free visit to God's zoo, but it is very much a zoo without walls or bars.

God's rhetorical questions focus on the awesome vastness of the cosmos and the power required to "operate" it (38.1-38),[19] then the earth's wildlife and its freedom (38.39–40.2). In response,

Job acknowledges his relative insignificance in three profound words: "I am small" (40.4).[20] After a second round of questioning, in which God refers to Behemoth and Leviathan, beasts of mythic proportion, Job "changes his mind" (traditionally, "repents"; 42.1-6). Before he has only heard of God, but now he "sees" God, and "changes his mind about dust and ashes" (i.e., about his mourning).[21] Job is ready to live again.

What has happened to produce this spiritual transformation? In seeing wild animals in all their freedom, *not* subject to human dominion and domestication, Job realizes that the world is far larger than his *own* little world (38.39-39.30). The lions—objects of human fear—are the objects of God's care. God feeds them, along with the ravens and its chicks who cry to God. Mountain goats and deer calve with only God as a midwife, and their young grow up free to roam wherever they want. The same wild freedom characterizes the ass, the ostrich, the hawk, and the eagle. Forced to look at the needs of animals for food, and how God cares for them, Job must suspend his ranting and raving, however justified it may be. God's questions demand that Job *pay attention* to the animal realm and its intrinsic worth. Instead of continuing his cries to God, Job must listen to the cries of the raven's chicks. Instead of hungering for justice, Job must empathize with their hunger for food. Indeed, for a moment he is invited to look at the world from *their* perspective rather than his own, anthropocentric perspective. That process of imaginative identification is also the beginning of spiritual transformation, because the cry of the chicks calls Job out of himself, opening the possibility that the one who returns from the wild will be a new person.

When Job says, "now my eye sees you" (42.5), "you" (God) includes the wild realm of nature. Here God's love is freely given to animals completely apart from any human connection. Here is "the grace of the world"[22] that exists beyond Job's fixation on what is right and wrong, on who is innocent and who is guilty, who is punished and who is rewarded. In glimpsing this world of divine gratuity, Job leaves behind the enormity of his pain and the "dust and ashes" of his complaints. Job abandons a "misguided speciesism"[23] and enters a realm of "deep ecology." Here the *reason* for his suffering goes unexplained, but Job is empowered to abandon his questions and embrace life anew. Now "Job can stand up, shake the dust off his feet, slough off his misconceptions, and run with the wild [animals]."[24]

The imagery in the whirlwind speeches suggests a number of connections with Oliver's poetry. God shows Job the awesome beauty of nature, but that beauty includes the terror of tooth and claw. God invites Job to watch the eagle soar, but also to see the vulture's "young ones suck up blood" (39.30).[25] Oliver shows us the vultures who "minister" to nature by devouring the bodies of the dead, thereby producing "the miracle: / resurrection" ("Vultures," AP 37; NSP 155). Again, God paints a detailed picture of Leviathan, most likely a crocodile (41.1–34), whose power and fearlessness make it without equal on earth, "king over all that are proud"—a final way of putting Job in his place. Oliver's "Alligator Poem" narrates her near-death encounter with the beast, after which she "saw the world as if for the second time, / the way it really is." Then she picks some lovely wild flowers, but holds them "in [her] trembling hands" (NSP 32).

In both Job and Oliver, it is the very wildness of animals that makes them a source of spiritual rejuvenation. As she says in her essay "Staying Alive," "And this is what I learned, that the world's otherness is antidote to confusion—that standing *within* this *otherness* can re-dignify the worst-stung heart" (BP 64).[26] "Do you observe the calving of the deer?" God asks Job. That is a rhetorical question expecting a negative answer, but Oliver can answer most affirmatively in "A Meeting" (AP 63; NSP 171):

> She steps into the dark swamp
> where the long wait ends.
>
> The secret slippery package
> drops to the weeds.
>
> She leans her long neck and tongues it
> between breaths slack with exhaustion
>
> and after a while it rises and becomes a creature
> like her, but much smaller.
>
> So now there are two. And they walk together
> like a dream under the trees.
>
> In early June, at the edge of a field
> thick with pink and yellow flowers

I meet them.
I can only stare.

She is the most beautiful woman
I have ever seen.

Her child leaps among the flowers,
the blue of the sky falls over me

like silk, the flowers burn, and I want
to live my life all over again, to begin again,

to be utterly
wild.

The title of the poem invokes a phenomenon introduced in our discussion of Buber above. Although our life is full of I-It experiences in which things (including people) are objects, to be truly alive one must enter into an I-Thou experience. The word unit I-It is "the word of separation." In contrast, as Buber says, "All real living is meeting." Indeed, we only realize our true identity as persons when we address other subjects as Thou.[27] In a sense, we are (re)created by relationship.

In "The Fawn," we heard Oliver sing to the deer; here she "can only stare," yet here too there is a "meeting." The mother deer drops her calf and then the calf "becomes a creature / like her." The language suggests an act of pro-creation.[28] The fawn "leaps among the flowers" and suddenly the "sky falls" and "the flowers burn," signaling an epiphany in which the poet is transformed: "and I want / to live my life all over again, to begin again, / to be utterly / wild." The procreation of the fawn produces a re-creation in the poet, the birth of the animal a rebirth of the human. Finally, as we saw with Job, Oliver identifies her spiritual rejuvenation as a return to wildness.[29]

Other poems about *fauna* resemble "A Meeting" in presenting a new beginning. In *Winter Hours* Oliver gives us an opportunity to see how she would want us to read a poem, in this case, "The Swan" (WH 27). Oliver says that every one of her poems "must have a spiritual purpose," and part of that purpose is to engage the reader as participant. The poem should "invite the reader to want to do something beyond merely receiving beauty" (WH 24). Indeed, the poem poses a challenge to readers to find their own answer to a question raised but left unanswered by the poet. The purpose of "the beautiful poem" is to "charge us with a difficult and ennobling task" (BP 115). In "The Swan," a swan comes gliding toward the poet, and the poem ends with a question: "Oh, what will I do, what will I say, when those / white wings / touch the shore?" The ending, she says, "is a closure yet it is also a moment of arrival, and therefore a possible new beginning" (WH 25).

A similar spiritual transformation occurs in another poem about an encounter with a deer, "Morning at Great Pond" (AP 46). Sunrise over the pond dissolves the night and "its craven doubt," the shimmering light "turning the ponds / to plates of fire." A deer stands in the water drinking, then turns and its motion ripples the water:

> the silver water
> crushes like silk,
> shaking the sky,
> and you're healed then
> from the night, your heart
> wants more, you're ready
> to rise and look!
> to hurry anywhere!
> to believe in everything.

Here the transformation is from illness to healing, from doubt to belief, and from apathy to attentiveness (again, one of Oliver's key words—"look!").

The poems that we have just looked at display a three-fold movement that takes place in the *fauna*, in the poet, and (ideally) in the reader. A deer gives birth, the poet is "born again," and the reader is invited to participate in the rebirth. These poems reveal an almost "evangelical" heuristic quality in that they seek to "convert" the reader into a fresh way of *looking* at the world that will lead the reader to her own spiritual transformation—or better, exploration, remembering that Oliver wants to pose questions rather than answers. In the same interrogative sense, we could summarize the movement in a poem that we have looked at already, "The Summer Day" (HL 60; NSP 94). Here the poet's attention ("how to pray") focuses on a grasshopper, prompted by the initial theological question "Who made the world?" but leading finally to an existential question addressed to the reader: "what is it you plan to do / with your one wild and precious life?"[30]

Such challenging questions constitute the "moral" of Oliver's poems, not in the sense of a proverb or maxim, but as a kind of ethical responsibility. To repeat, she wants the reader "to *do* something beyond merely *receiving* beauty" (my emphasis). In her essays, Oliver states that she is not really an environmentalist in that her poems do not try to persuade people to protect the earth (*WH* 99). However, it is impossible to imagine that an appropriate response to the arrival of the swan would be to catch it and wring its neck, or that the blessing tree would be more useful as lumber, or that the fawn's head would look nice stuffed and mounted on the wall. If the woods is a temple, one would think twice about bulldozing it and hauling it away in a dump truck—unless, of course, one has "gone crazy / for power, / for things" ("The Sun," *NSP* 50).[31] Even if Oliver herself does not take the step, surely one of the most important things for us to *do* is to find ways to *preserve* the beauty that we see in her poems, that is, the beauty of the world.

Oliver's comments on the way she intends her poems to move from looking at nature to questioning the reader bear a striking resemblance to some hermeneutical discussions among biblical scholars and theologians. In other words, there is a remarkable correspondence between her way of reading the Other Book of God, and at least one way of reading the biblical book of God.

In a groundbreaking work, Walter Wink traced the interpretive process that leads to, as his title succinctly expresses, *The Bible in Human Transformation*.[32] Wink followed a development in interpretive perspective that leads from an unquestioning acceptance of the truth claims of the text, to a critical objectification of the text, to a mutual relationship between reader and text in which each questions the other. I as reader am both subject and object, as is the text itself. That is, the text addresses me just as much as I address the text. Wink puts it this way:

> As knower I know that in the knowledge gained
> of the object I am first of all known. There is here
> an unveiling through the object that discloses to
> me a depth beyond my reckoning, a depth through
> which I begin to be released from egocentric
> stratagems and reunited with all creation.[33]

A similar interpretation appears in one of Thomas Merton's books. Merton paraphrases a famous comment of Karl Barth, who said, "When you begin to question the Bible you find that the Bible is also questioning you. When you ask: 'What is this book?' you find that you are also implicitly being asked: 'Who is this that reads it?'"[34] In fact, one of Merton's comments reminds us immediately of the challenging question at the end of "The Summer Day" ("what do you plan to do . . . ?"): "If we ask [the Bible] for information about the meaning of life, it answers by asking us when we intend to start living?"[35] Similarly, we recall Oliver's description of her own authorial intent when Merton says that the Bible "challenges the reader and demands of him a personal engagement, a decision and commitment of his freedom, a judgment regarding an ultimate question."[36]

In short, when we compare the two books of God we can see that both function to ask the reader, Who are you and how do you intend to live? In reading both we encounter holiness, we receive a blessing, we are healed, we are reborn. Just as Wink can talk about the Bible in human transformation, so Oliver could talk about "Nature in Human Transformation." She brings us to the temple in the wildwood and challenges us "to believe in everything," to "begin again," to "look!"

FOUR

Animate Inanima

Storms are fine speakers and tell all they know,
but their voices of lightning, torrent, and rushing
wind are infinitely less numerous than their
nameless still small voices too low for human
ears; and because we are poor listeners we fail to
catch much that is even fairly within reach.
(John Muir, *Nature Writings*, 612)

1. Storm

Within a few years of Martin Buber's *I and Thou*, Rudolf Otto published a book entitled *The Idea of the Holy*. Otto was interested in a dimension of the holy that was different from its association with moral goodness as well as intellectual concepts. For this dimension he coined the term *numinous*, from the Latin *numen*, which signified divine power and majesty. In a numinous experience, people encounter an overwhelming power that produces a number of reactions, most fundamentally the combination of fear and fascination. The aspect of the holy corresponding to these subjective reactions Otto dubbed *mysterium tremendum et fascinans* (some things just sound better in Latin). When people encounter the holy they are overcome with fear, which may range from the negative side of horror to the positive side of sublime awe.[1] But the element of fear is always there, analogous to a sense of the uncanny. The holy is "wholly *other*," absolutely unapproachable. Yet, at the same time, the holy is utterly fascinating. It attracts the very person that it also overpowers. An outstanding biblical example is Moses' encounter with God at the burning bush. Moses cannot help but turn aside to see the great wonder, yet when he hears the voice he is afraid to look (Exod 3.1–5; cf. Gen 28.10–12, 16–17; Isaiah 6). Otto suggested that the experience of the numinous "forms the starting-point for the entire religious development in history."[2]

Some of the most perdurable religious motifs for the numinous derive from the thunderstorm. To ancient peoples, thunderstorms were the most powerful occurrences in nature (next to earthquakes, perhaps). The power of the storm was seen and felt in the dark clouds and wind, rain or hail, booming thunder and flashing lightning. The storm's power is raw, elemental, untamed—frightening and exhilarating at the same time, like Otto's "wholly other." The power was more than meteorological—it was theological. The power of the storm was *divine* power. In the Ancient Near East, storm gods were prominent in virtually every culture, including ancient Israel. The imagery appears in the Bible ("the Lord thundered in the heaven, and the Most High uttered his voice," Ps 18.13), is repeated in contemporary hymns ("see the cloud and fire appear"),[3] and even survives in Santa Claus's sleigh (pulled by reindeer named Donner and Blitzen, German for "thunder" and "lightning," respectively).[4] Ambivalent in its affects, the storm could cause destruction, and yet it was the source of the fertility of the land. To borrow a phrase from Annie Dillard, the storm was "grace tangled in a rapture with violence."[5]

Otto's delineation of the numinous, and the storm god of ancient religions, will help us see the spiritual dimensions of four of Oliver's poems about storms. She has also written a prose description of a storm, but because the latter also involves a storm-tossed sea, we will postpone looking at it until we look at the sea itself, and how storm and sea are linked together.

In "Lightning" (AP 7; NSP 146), Oliver describes a storm as a "shapeless mouth" that howls for five hours, something like the banshee, that legendary Gaelic spirit whose wail presages death. The wind snaps tree branches, cutting off electric power and plunging everything into darkness. Every now and then the lightning flashes, momentarily illuminating the landscape like a cosmic flashbulb. So startling is this reappearance of the world out of blackness that it is "like a quick / lesson in creation," evoking the biblical image of primeval darkness giving way to light (Gen 1.1-3).

Having described the scene outside, the poem turns inside, describing the reaction of those who huddle in the house.

as always,
it was hard to tell
fear from excitement:
how sensual
the lightning's
poured stroke! and still,
what a fire and a risk!
As always the body
wants to hide,
wants to flow toward it—strives
to balance while
fear shouts,
excitement shouts, back
and forth. . .

Oliver's description of the storm here clearly reflects the kind of numinous experience outlined by Otto. In particular, the power exhibited by lightning is both fascinating and fearsome. Oliver's description of the experience is more somatic than cerebral—the lightning's "poured stroke" (perhaps like a ribbon of molten lava) is "sensual"; the human reaction appears in "the body" more than the brain.[6] Although the poet's words beautifully name the experience, the immediate reaction to the encounter is a gut response. The lightning triggers something primitive, something deeper than words or concepts.[7]

Although it goes unsaid in "Lightning," danger is the companion of the storm's fearsomeness, as is often the case with a numinous experience. In "Storm in Massachusetts, September 1982" (DW 71), this danger comes to the surface. In addition to lightning, other storm phenomena appear—clouds, wind, and thunder. Suddenly, despite "a clear heaven" overhead, a thunderstorm appears "over the horizon" with its dark clouds and distant thunder. Just as suddenly, the poet thinks of her "good life" and "of other lives / / being blown apart." The storm appears as sheer threat, an ominous, destructive power that in an instant can turn people's lives upside down. The poem reflects the reality of a world in which a tornado can appear from nowhere and in seconds toss mobile homes into the air, killing their inhabitants.

"Storm in Massachusetts" speaks of the fragility and precariousness of life and the ever-present possibility of death, and a violent death at that. It is a lesson in mortality, another example of the dark side, the "terror," in Oliver's poetry that we have seen before.

•:•

> life is much the same
> 　　when it's going well—
> 　　resonant
> 　　　　and unremarkable.
> But who,
> 　　not under disaster's seal,
> 　　can understand what life is like
> 　　when it begins to crumble?

With this somber reflection, Oliver turns again to focus on the approaching storm, its "drumming" noise advancing against her "safe" situation. Now the sound is even more menacing: the "rounds of thunder . . . / sound / like gunfire."[8]

The tension between complacency and danger evident in "Storm in Massachusetts" appears in a different form in "Beyond the Snow Belt" (*NSP* 245). Again the poem opens with an ominous tone: "Over the local stations, one by one, / announcers list disasters like dark poems / That always happen in the skull of winter." But then we see people living blithely where the snow is both beautiful and benign—children playing, adults smiling. They are not mindful of those, just two counties to the north, for whom the snowstorm has brought death. They "Forget with ease each far mortality." While Oliver says that she does not wish to excuse such apparent insensitivity, she concludes that "except as we have loved, / All news arrives as from a distant land."

If "Beyond the Snow Belt" is about our forgetfulness of mortality, "Storm" (*TM* 59) presents a frozen world that appears inimical to humans but inert to animals. The opening stanzas trace the plummeting thermometer down below zero "To the dark side / Of winter." Then comes an oblique reference to God, hinted at by a common expression that usually has no serious theological content: "Heaven / Help us! I say. But heaven / Is full of spitting snow." If heaven does evoke its resident here, it is not a pretty picture. Heaven spits in your face! But then the poem turns to the animal world. Deer, foxes, and crows

> Are beginning to shiver. But they
>
> Can bear the wrack of the storm. Patient
> As stones or leaves or clumps of clay,
> What saves them is not knowing they are mortal—

What saves them is thinking that dying
Is only floating away into
The life of the snow.

This is one of numerous poems in which Oliver deals with the ambiguity of death. Here death is implied in the deepening cold. To us it is threatening and insulting—spitting in our face—but to animals it is nothing because they do not *know* that they are mortal. For them death is only the entrance into another form of life. As elsewhere, Oliver leaves us pondering what she means. Should we learn the lesson from animals that death is really not the threat that it seems? Should we welcome death as the transition to another dimension of reality? Or, instead, is the intimation of immortality a naïve fantasy, and the finality of death inescapable? We can ask the same questions of other poems about waterfalls and hawks.[9]

In these poems about storms, one of nature's most powerful forces reveals the fragility of life, the capricious danger that lurks just over the horizon, and the imminent possibility of death. While there are allusions to religious tradition (creation out of darkness, heaven as a source of salvation), the poems do not pursue an explicitly theological intent. However, in confronting us with the ultimate "limit situation"—our mortality—the poems invite us to explore the spiritual meaning of our lives. Oliver's attention to the book of nature in some ways resembles what we may also read in the book of Scripture. Human life is "like a flower of the field; / for the wind passes over it, and it is gone, and its place knows it no more" (Ps 103.15-16).

As we have seen before, Oliver's attention to nature does not flinch from the "dark side" of storms, a phrase used literally in "Beyond the Snow Belt." There is no sentimentalism here. Indeed, it is the very destructive power of storms that makes them so awesome. A gentle rain, with no thunder and lightning and no wind, does not instill that "terror" of nature that is a major theme in Oliver's work. Storms present contemporary human beings with one of the forces of nature that is beyond our control, before which we must stand helpless, and from which we must flee. Although we can predict storms and therefore be forewarned, our inability to control them makes us little different from our ancient ancestors. Here too storms present us with the limitations within which we must live, and in the wake of their destruction, they point to a power that far transcends human beings.

•:•

One of the films that I remember from my childhood was called *Creature from the Black Lagoon*. I have only a vague recollection of it now, but I know it included horrifying scenes in which a dragon-like creature would emerge from the water, devour a few humans, and return, until the hero destroyed it. Next to *Jurassic Park* or *The Lord of the Rings* the technical effects would seem tame, but at the time the monster was convincing enough. The film *Jaws*, too, was so terrifying that many viewers had difficulty swimming in the ocean. In fact, as I was writing these lines shark attacks on humans along the Eastern seaboard prompted this sentence in *Time* Magazine: "Sharks lurk in the vast, mysterious ocean, an element that still stirs mythic fear."[10]

The mythic association between the sea and a monster is as old as recorded history. One of the myths from Mesopotamia, *Enuma elish* ("When on high"), tells of the creation of the world that results from a struggle for power among the gods. The villain is the sea, personified as a monster, Tiamat. The hero is Marduk, the chief god of the Babylonian pantheon and patron deity of the city-state of Babylon. Marduk is a storm deity armed with weapons including lightning, winds, storm, and cloud chariot. In the battle, Marduk defeats Tiamat, and from her dismembered body he constructs the universe and makes humans from the blood of one of Tiamat's generals. All of the gods proclaim Marduk their king, and they construct the city of Babylon, along with Marduk's temple. The order of heaven and earth is established.[11]

And yet, it is *not* established. Near the end of the epic, the gods say of Marduk, "May he vanquish Tiamat; may her life be strait and short! / Into the future of mankind, when days have grown old, / May she recede without cease and stay away forever."[12] Despite Marduk's definitive victory, Tiamat—the sea—remains a constant threat. One day, instead of receding, she may advance, threatening the world with chaos once again. When the Babylonians recited the epic every year at their New Year festival, they thus acknowledged the sovereignty of Marduk but also, as it were, Tiamat's lingering ghost.

Change the name of the hero (along with other significant differences), and you will see versions of *Enuma elish* throughout the Bible, literally from beginning (Genesis) to end (Revelation). Sometimes the references are little more than allusions to the sea as a threat, but at other times the dragon itself appears: "God my king is from of old, / working salvation in the earth. / You divided the sea by your might; / you broke the heads of the dragons in the waters, / You crushed the heads of Leviathan" (Ps 74.12–14a). The biblical references to the combat story suggest ambivalence similar to that in the *Enuma elish*. As the title of a major study says, the problem is that of *Creation and the Persistence of Evil*.[13] On the one hand, God defeated the dragon at the dawn of creation. On the other hand, the persistence of the combat motif suggests that, like the Babylonians, Israel struggled with the continuing reality of a threat to their security, represented by the sea monster.

It would be an exaggeration to suggest that the ancient myth of the sea continues in Oliver's writings. Nevertheless, in two of her works, the sea, combined with storm, appears as a menacing power that—shorn of explicit religious references—we might call the twin sibling of Tiamat.

In the opening lines of "The Waves" (DW 66), Oliver immediately dispenses with the notion of sea as a simple geographical term: "The sea / isn't a place / but a fact, and / a mystery." In the second stanza, Oliver locates the mystery "under its [the sea's] green and black / cobbled coat that never / stops moving." It may go too far for us to associate this image with the mythical dragon (instead of "cobbled coat" she does *not* say, after all, "scaled skin"). But at least we may see here a creature-like being that is dark, perpetually agitated, and, most of all, potentially lethal, for the closing line of the stanza is "When death," thereby linking the menace of the sea to the subject of "disaster" that follows.

The phrase "When death" introduces a change in point-of-view from sea to land. Oliver evokes the common phenomenon of a fatal car accident, how passersby slow down to gawk and imagine what it would be like to be the victim. Immediately she returns to the sea and the moment immediately following a storm, how the fishermen set out to do their work. Then she says, "Surely the sea / / is the most beautiful fact / in our universe, but / you won't find a fisherman / who will say so." Here again is Oliver's theme of the inextricability of nature's beauty and terror, like "the beauty / of the blue shark cruising toward the tumbling seals" ("Cold Poem," AP 31). Fishermen refuse to acknowledge the beauty because they know the terror, so all they will say is *"See you later"* (italics hers). That is a wishful parting, perhaps even a bit superstitious. Yet their fear is justified, for despite the sea's beauty, in the end "the bones / / of the drowned fisherman / are returned, half a year later, / in the glittering, / laden nets." The sea has claimed another victim.[14]

In the ancient Near Eastern mythology, the storm often appears as the weapon of the storm god and is used against the sea as the enemy. In "The Waves," however, the storm and sea appear as a combined force, at once beautiful and terrifying. The awesome combination of the sea's "mystery" reminds us once again of Otto's *mysterium tremendum* and the numinous.[15]

"The sea / isn't a place / but a fact, and / a mystery." "Fact" here seems to mean something like "the way things are." "Fact" is "what life is like" *both* "when it's going well" and "when it begins to crumble," as we saw in "Storm in Massachusetts." Not surprisingly, there is a close relationship between the themes in "The Waves" and in Oliver's poems about storms. Both sea and storm represent the precariousness and fragility of human existence, a "fact" that we must accept if our appreciation of nature's beauty is to be realistic rather than sentimental. "The sea / / is the most beautiful fact / in our universe, but" those who are wise will not count on life's benevolence; they will say—hopefully— "see you later."

In an essay titled "Winter Hours," Oliver also presents a description of a storm over the ocean as it approaches the shore (WH 103–105).[16] The onslaught of the swirling surf is both "beautiful and dreadful." The sea is "all darkness that rises." The swirling waters churn up aquatic animals, providing dinner for the eiders, but the ducks and gulls have fled. The howling wind and pounding surf together seem to envelop the world from above and below. The course of the storm is relentless. "The ranks of the waves . . . never stop coming. For hours it continues: still dreadful, still beautiful." The advance of the sea is "frightening," a "peril for anything so minor as a house, or so breakable as a human person." Yet there is also "something strangely peaceful"—"the spirit senses that purest of mysteries: power without anger, injury without malice." Then again Oliver repeats the phrase "beautiful and dreadful."

Oliver's description ends on a wonderfully ambivalent note. The sea is at "full flood." Now personified and speaking, it has advanced into her yard, but there it abruptly stops, and says "*Not this time,* and, still screaming, but with each wave a less dreadful scream, it began to descend" (italics hers). Oliver then begins the next section of her essay with a transitional look back: "So the storm passed, that one."

Just as the ancient world used the threatening sea to acknowledge the "persistence of evil," so here and in "The Waves" Oliver uses the sea to expose the "fact" of life's precariousness, the "dreadful" that must be seen along with the "beautiful." Indeed, the final image in the prose description, that of a screaming creature that stops just short of annihilation, and the author's final words about the storm ("that one") suggesting that the ultimate threat yet remains, seem to represent a contemporary albeit "demythologized" version of the ancient combat theme with its rich irresolution. It is as if in Oliver we see the experiential starting point for the ancient mythology, the encounter with the numinous power of the sea that would lead eventually to a figure like Tiamat or Leviathan (cf. "Alligator Poem," NSP 32). Yet, of course, there remain significant differences, not the least of which is that nowhere does Oliver speak of a divine "hero" figure. In the closing lines of the prose description, the sea says "thus far and no further," to use the words of Job 38.11, whereas in Job it is God who imposes the limit. At least in the works cited, for Oliver there is no "savior" figure to whom we may appeal.

And yet, maybe there is, to pursue the title of another intriguing poem, "Maybe" (HL 76; NSP 97). This is one of Oliver's infrequent poems dealing explicitly with religious subjects, in this case, the story of Jesus' stilling the storm (Mt 8.23–27). In the opening stanza, when Jesus stands up in the boat, "the sea lay down, / / silky and sorry." The sea is something like a domesticated animal that has gotten out of line and now regrets it. Both the New Testament story and Oliver's poem mirror the Hebrew Bible's mythic language, as in Ps 104.6–7: "at your rebuke [the deep and waters] flee." Moreover, as in the ancient myth, in "Maybe" there is a hero figure, Jesus, by whose words "everybody was saved."

Jesus' status of savior, however, is ephemeral, Oliver suggests. People quickly return to everyday preoccupations once the spectacular recedes. So it is with the soul. "Nobody knows what the soul is. / / It comes and goes / like the wind over the water." Only at certain extraordinary moments do a few people feel "the soul slip forth," as after Jesus' sermon on the mount, or after his feeding the multitude. But now the exhausted disciples are asleep in the boat. They have forgotten

how the wind tore at the sails
before he rose and talked to it—

tender and luminous and demanding
as he always was—
a thousand times more frightening
than the killer sea.

Here the "sweet Jesus" of the opening line suddenly becomes
a figure who is both "tender" and terrifying, and the sea becomes
the "killer" that we know from "The Waves." At least in this one
instance, "maybe" there *is* a divine figure, a numinous power that
can tame the raging sea.

"May [Tiamat] recede without cease and stay away forever,"
says the ancient Babylonian myth. "Thus far you shall come, and
no further," says God to the sea. "*Not this time*, and, still scream-
ing, but with each wave a less dreadful scream, it began to
descend," writes the contemporary poet. Stretching across thou-
sands of years these texts reveal the numinous quality of storm
and sea, two of nature's most formidable subjects. In each text—
the Babylonian, the biblical, and the modern—there is the human
fear of disaster that haunts our lives. In a sense, all of us are like
the child who is afraid of the monster that lurks in the darkness
under her bed, partly because we have seen what the monster
can do. And yet there lives in us the remembrance of and the
hope for a savior who will conquer the Deep.[17]

Dirty Book

I<small>F MAN WERE ONLY MIND</small>, worship in thought would be the form in which to commune with God. But man is body and soul, and his goal is so to live that both "his heart and his flesh should sing to the living God." (Abraham Heschel, *God in Search of Man*, 297 [paraphrasing Psalm 78.4])

I don't want you just to sit down at the table.
I don't want you just to eat, and be content.
I want you to walk out into the fields
where the water is shining, and the rice has risen.
I want you to stand there, far from the white tablecloth.
I want you to fill your hands with the mud, like a blessing.

The book of nature—the Other Book of God—is a dirty book. That such a description at first sight appears to be pejorative is a sad irony to which we shall return in a moment. But here, in the poem called "Rice" (*NSP* 38), Oliver rubs our noses in the dirt. In the beginning of the poem, she describes how the rice grows "in the black mud." Oliver invites us to recover the intimacy between the earth and ourselves. Most of us are far removed from the source of the food we eat. Not only do we not grow it, or even know *how* it is grown, but also some of it comes from faraway countries, like the rice of Southeast Asia. We haven't planted it, picked it, milled it, or packaged it. The hand that holds the fork has never touched a plow or a rake or the grain on the stalk, much less the earth in which the stalk grows. Oliver seems to suggest that we can't really appreciate food as a blessing unless we get in touch with the dirt out of which it comes. We have to move from the "white tablecloth," with all of its clean separation from the source of food, and "fill [our] hands with the mud," the "black mud" without which we would have no use for the tablecloth. In order to be fully literate in the book of nature, we have to "get down and dirty."[1]

The dirtiness of the Other Book of God should not surprise us. Our preceding survey of Oliver's poetry has prepared us for the grace hidden in dirtiness. Recall "Skunk Cabbage" (AP 44; NSP 160), in which Oliver is in search of lovely spring flowers but, instead, encounters the cabbage, sticking up "through the chilly mud." The plant emits a lurid smell from its ugly leaves, but out of its "thick root nested below" in the dirt, the miracle of "life again" is reenacted. Or think of "Crossing the Swamp" (AP 58; NSP 166), a metaphor for the way in which we seem to get stuck in the mud yet can emerge like a spring bud. Just as genuine enjoyment of rice requires getting your hands dirty, so true rejuvenation often requires getting your feet muddy.

Rice—indeed, all food—is holy because it is a blessing. Blessing in the biblical traditions manifests itself in material things—fertility, bountiful crops, ample food and drink, and peaceful relationships—even a little money to set aside (e.g., Deut 8.7-9, 12-13). The Psalmist praises God as "very great" because God provides food for humans and beasts alike, in particular "wine to gladden the human heart, / oil to make the face shine, / and bread to strengthen the human heart" (Ps 104.15). Here bread is sacred not because it is the unleavened bread of Passover, or because it is the bread blessed by Jesus at the Last Supper—both such hallowings based on historical events. Here bread (and oil and wine) is sacred because it is simply essential for life. In other words, bread is a blessing, and holy, because it is a product of nature (and ultimately, of course, of the creator) and is essential for human existence. Bread as blessing involves the natural process in which plants emerge from the dirt, grow, and bear fruit. Like bread, the rice of Oliver's poem is the kind of blessing that you can put on the table, precisely what one would expect from the "god of dirt."

Another way to describe the holiness of food is to say that it has a sacramental dimension. According to one traditional definition, a sacrament is something visible and tangible that conveys an invisible and intangible grace. However, that definition tends to disassociate grace from the very materiality of the medium. But the "blessing" of rice is inextricably tied up in the nutrition that sustains life. In that sense, rice is holy because it is food, plain and simple, not because it represents "spiritual food." As Larry Rasmussen puts it, sacramentalism "recognizes and celebrates the divine in, with, and under all nature, ourselves included," and is "sometimes called 'panentheism.'"[2] Panentheism is not pantheism, however; the latter identifies nature with God, the former finds God *in* nature, but not limited thereby. As Rasmussen says, "To identify something earthly as holy and sacred is not to say it *is* God. Rather, it is *of* God; God is present in its presence."[3] The Catholic tradition recognizes seven sacraments; Protestants, by and large, only two. Perhaps the "reformation" should have been in the other direction, namely, *expanding* the number rather than contracting. Otherwise, as one theologian says, we risk "the theological belittling of daily food for the body."[4]

We can construe Oliver's reading of the Other Book of God as a sacramental reading. In fact, as she watches a heron feed on frogs, she draws an explicit connection between Eucharistic bread and our everyday food.

> . . . didn't Jesus say:
> "This is my body,"
> meaning, the bread—
> and meaning, also,
>
> the things of this world?
> . . . .
> It is the hard
>
> and terrible truth
> we live with,
> feeding ourselves
> every day. ("Blue Heron," *WP* 20)

As she watches the little frogs sliding down head first into the gullet of the heron, Oliver again addresses what she calls "the hard / / and terrible truth" involved in all feeding (cf. Chapter 2). For one creature to survive, another must be broken and eaten. Then she turns to human eating and invokes the Eucharistic words of Jesus, implying that *all* eating is in some sense an extension of the sacramental partaking of the body of Christ. As in "Rice," everyday food is a blessing, but here Oliver appeals explicitly to religious tradition to express the meaning and significance of that blessing. For some Christians, Oliver's poem might constitute an unorthodox Eucharistic theology in which the story of Jesus' last supper loses its unique historical configuration. Nevertheless, if we can understand Jesus' words ("This is my body") as an expression of the incarnation of God in him, but not *only* in him, then our everyday "feeding" is at least a sacrament of the same divine presence that is in the Eucharist. According to Rasmussen, such seems to be the implication of Martin Luther when he writes, regarding just those Eucharistic words, "God in his essence is present everywhere in and through the whole creation in all its parts and in all places, and so the world is full of God and God fills it all, yet God is not limited to or circumscribed by it, but is at the same time beyond and above the whole of creation."[5] The extension of the Eucharistic words to include all food also has ethical and political dimensions. Ecological theology merges with economic theology. In his book *God the Economist,* M. Douglas Meeks says, "When Jesus takes, blesses, breaks, and gives bread, he is explaining the shared communal meaning of the social *good,* bread. . . . The celebration of the Lord's Supper . . . [has] implications for all eating and drinking everywhere." When Jesus commands the disciples to eat, "it includes the command that they should share daily bread with all of God's people."[6]

Daily bread, then, is not simply a symbol of blessing; it *is* a blessing—one that you can see, smell, touch, taste, and eat. Unlike dogmas or creeds or catechisms, sacraments are *sensed,* and nature is a sensual book, as well as a dirty book. To recall a key theme— paying attention—one does not simply attend *mentally* to what one sees in nature; rather, one must apprehend nature with all of the senses. Attention must be a bodily engagement. Here quite literally Oliver the poet seems to *embody* a philosophy of language. As David Abram says, "the heart of even our most abstract cogitations [is] the sensuous and sentient life of the body itself."[7] The sensuality of nature's book is central to "The Plum Trees" (AP 84):

> Such richness flowing
> through the branches of summer and into
>
> the body, carried inward on the five
> rivers! Disorder and astonishment
>
> rattle your thoughts and your heart
> cries for rest but don't
>
> succumb, there's nothing
> so sensible as sensual inundation. Joy
> is a taste before
> it's anything else, and the body

can lounge for hours devouring
the important moments. Listen,

the only way
to tempt happiness into your mind is by taking it

into the body first, like small
wild plums.

"The Plum Trees" is indeed a sensual poem that we easily could have included in the chapter on *flora*. Nature's "richness" flows from the ground into and through the tree's branches and the fruit, on into the body of the poet. The tree literally and figuratively *feeds* her. It is none other than "joy" and "happiness" that the tree imparts, two of the greatest of spiritual gifts. The poem is a "thanksgiving" (*eucharist*) for the "fruit of the ground" (Deut 26:2, 10).[8]

Here again we see Oliver's "astonishment" at nature's wonder, accompanied now by disorientation: "Disorder . . . / rattle[s] your thoughts." Nature's richness creates cognitive dissonance, but the result is not so much mental confusion as it is a shift to a somatic perspective. It is "the five / rivers"—the five senses— that bear the richness. The sensible *becomes* sensual, inundated with joy, and it is the body that *senses* joy and happiness before the mind can conceive of them. The body *tastes* them, just as it tastes the "wild plums" of the tree. Similarly, in "August" (AP 3; NSP 143), Oliver brings us to blackberry picking. In the center of the poem she finds herself "thinking / / of nothing." Here again what is sensible is sensual. While her mind comes to a stop, her *sense of taste* is in high gear, "cramming / the black honey of summer / into my mouth." In the end, it is her "happy tongue" through which "my body / / accepts what it is."[9] That Oliver's "taste" can be literal as well as figurative appears in a remarkable disclosure of just how willing she is to identify with the animal world: she joins kittens in suckling their mother's milk (BP 65).

"There's nothing / so sensible as sensual inundation." Much of Western thought has avoided such an equation between the sensible and the sensual. After all, for most people, the word "sensible" refers to an explanation that appeals to reason; rational, convincing evidence is what we need for something to "make sense." The sensible and the sensual then join with other pairs of opposites: body/soul, flesh/spirit, matter/mind, feeling/ thinking. Although biblical traditions affirm the inseparability of

•:•

body and spirit (see below), subsequent interpretations easily saw a dichotomy in appeals to live "in the Spirit" and not "in the flesh" (e.g., Rom 8.9).[10] Add the Greek notion of an immortal soul imprisoned in the body and you can end up with that old evangelical song "I'll Fly Away" when it says, "like a bird from prison bars has flown." Then bring in Rene Descartes and his famous dictum "I think therefore I am," and the distinction between *mind* and body only increases—and we haven't even mentioned sex. As James Nelson points out, the result is a situation in which "the body and its sensations, which *seem* to belong to the natural world more than to history, are religiously suspect."[11] In "Wild Geese," (*DW* 14; *NSP* 110) Oliver rejects religious mortification of the body that requires self-inflicted pain. Instead, redemption comes from realizing one's bodily "place / in the family of things":

> You do not have to be good.
> You do not have to walk on your knees
> for a hundred miles through the desert, repenting.
> You only have to let the soft animal of your body
>   love what it loves.

The suspicion of the body extends to the material world, i.e., to nature. Just as people often assume that what is "sensual" is automatically sexual, so what is "dirty" is sinful. The use of "dirt" to symbolize sin, of course, is one of the most primitive expressions of fault.[12] The antonym is "cleanness," as in the proverb "cleanliness is next to godliness." Nevertheless, the association between dirt and sinfulness easily becomes as damaging as that between *body* and sinfulness. To illustrate, one need only think of the lurid fantasies one might conjure up in hearing that the Other Book of *God* is a dirty, sensual book.

As numerous scholars have increasingly pointed out, the dichotomy between mind and matter, body and soul, spirit and flesh has come to haunt us. Beneficial though this dichotomy has been, especially in the development of modern science, the division between the spiritual and the physical has proved to be harmful to our understanding of spirituality, and, ironically, not reflective of the very physical world that science addresses.[13] Moreover, as the quotation from Heschel at the head of this chapter suggests, in biblical anthropology human beings are *not* "only mind," and therefore we cannot limit worship to "thought." We are also "heart and flesh," so we must sing as well as think.[14] As theologian Diogenes Allen says, "Body and soul are so intimate that they are more than united. The body is the soul in its outward manifestation."[15] "There's nothing / so sensible as sensual inundation." In that one line alone, Oliver bridges the gap between mind and body, and, as if to compensate for long neglect, gives the body pride of place.

Because the Other Book of God is a dirty, sensual book, we will find the spiritual in the dirt and the sensuality, rather than apart from them. For what we might call "deep sacramentalism," the material does not simply *point to* the spiritual. The spiritual is *in* the material. To recall our reading of "The Fawn" (TM 13) when Oliver asks "Oh what is holiness?" We find that the answer is not some reality *beyond* her encounter with the fawn. As Rasmussen says (above), "God is present in its presence."[16] Holiness is wrapped up in the "meeting" of poet and animal in all their physicality.

The combination of dirt (as "matter") and "spirit" becomes explicit in "Poem" (DW 52). "The spirit / likes to dress up like this: / ten fingers, / ten toes, / / shoulders, and all the rest," the latter including the "branches / of the world." The spirit "could float, of course," as most popular notions of spirit suggest—remaining an immaterial, weightless ghost-like being. But the spirit prefers to

> plumb rough matter.
>   Airy and shapeless thing,
>   it needs
>   the metaphor of the body

As we saw in Chapter 1 with regard to the heavens "talking," metaphors are the only means to represent certain realities, and surely that is true of spirit. A familiar hymn says that God is "in light inaccessible, hid from our eyes," and while that may express the transcendence of God, Oliver rather thinks of the spirit as "more than pure light / that burns / where no one is," because spirit "needs the body's world," and appears there. "So," she says, "it enters us" and "lights up" "the body / like a star."[17]

Another analogy to the appearance of spirit in the guise of ten toes or the branches of a tree is the notion of incarnation, the word becoming flesh (the biblical paradigm is John 1.14). Here spirit and matter are fused within history "instead of supplying the liberation from the material world that the Greek mind yearned for."[18] As Abram puts it philosophically, "the 'life-world'

⁘

. . . [is] a profoundly *carnal* field."[19] The Eastern Orthodox tradition of icons presents a particular example of how the doctrine of incarnation can connect us with nature. Tilden Edwards notes that "Sacred icons are rooted in the Incarnation."[20] An icon has the capacity to mediate a "spirit-body integration" in the observer *if* the observer becomes a *participant* rather than an objective onlooker. Edwards then offers an exercise for "praying through an icon." Normally, of course, these icons depict images of people deemed holy (Christ, Mary, other saints). But Edwards concludes with a suggestion of how to apply the exercise to nature: "Let every visible sight potentially become an icon . . . as you drop through your normal way of being present to people, trees, stones, etc., and sense them as latent transparencies for God."[21] Just as nature plays a sacramental role in Oliver's poetry, so we could say that nature functions as an icon, providing "latent transparencies" for the "god of dirt."

We can also compare the "spirit-body integration" to which Edwards refers with what Oliver calls the "sense of well-being." In "May" (AP 53), just as the bees dive into the spring flowers for food, so Oliver dives into them for "their spiritual honey." The flowers are "mute"—they cannot speak—yet they offer "the deepest certainty" that

> this sense of well-being, the flourishing
> of the physical body—rides
> near the hub of the miracle that everything
> is a part of, is as good
> as a poem or a prayer. . . .

The "sense of well-being" is arguably the goal of virtually all spiritual or religious traditions. "Well-being" is the meaning of *shalom;* "salvation" derives from the Latin *salus,* "health, soundness;" to be in harmony with the Tao provides serenity. For Oliver, *sensing* the "well-being" rooted in our physical body is the equivalent of prayer, just as is attention to nature.

These poems on "the sense of well-being" provide a fitting conclusion to our reading of the Other Book of God through Oliver's eyes. Without sentimentality, she has forced us to look at the unpleasant aspects of nature if we are to appreciate its beauty. Even a sharp little whiff of skunk odor (as opposed to its full unleashing) is a reminder "that love itself, without its pain, would be / no more than a shruggable comfort."[22] As with smell, so with taste: Even the sensuous enjoyment of juicy, wild blackberries requires Oliver to endure "ripped arms" suffered in the act of berry-picking (*AP* 3; *NSP* 143). But *through* the pain of the blackberry vines, "there is / this happy tongue," inviting us to taste, taste, taste, just as she has elsewhere bid us "look, look, look!" The reward that awaits us is inestimable, as she says in "May" (above) because reading this earthy, sensual, book of God has brought us to "the hub of the miracle that everything / is a part of." But one should not end a sentence, much less a book, with a preposition, so, astonished again by the "god of dirt," let us join in Oliver's prayer:

> Now we are awake
> and now we are come together
> and now we are thanking the Lord.
>
> This is easy,
> for the Lord is everywhere.
>
> He is in the water and the air,
> He is in the very walls.
>
> He is around us and in us.
> He is the floor on which we kneel.
>
> We make our songs for him
> as sweet as we can
>
> for his goodness,
> and, lo, he steps into the song
>
> and out of it, having blessed it,
> having recognized our intention,
>
> having awakened us, who thought we were awake,
> a second time,
> having married us to the air and the water,
>
> having lifted us in intensity,
> having lowered us in beautiful amiability,
>
> having given us
> each other,

•:•

and the weeds, dogs, cities, boats, dreams
that are the world.
["Her Grave, Again: 7. *(Matins)*" WK 51-52]

Notes to Preface

1. Written by Alvin Pitcher with the subtitle *Cultivating Creation Communities* (Cleveland: Pilgrim, 1993).
2. Written by William E. Gramley (St. Louis: Christian Board of Publication, 1988).
3. In a poem called "The Peace of Wild Things," a virtual companion to Psalm 23, in *Collected Poems* (New York: North Point, 1984), 69.

Notes to Introduction

1. Douglas Burton-Christie, "Nature, Spirituality, and Imagination in the Poetry of Mary Oliver," *CrossCurrents*, Spring, 1996, 99.
2. Again, such references increase in her most recent work. For examples, see LC 9–10, 49–50, 52–53; WK 51–52; OF 34.
3. Sermon 68,6. I thank Father Allan D. Fitzgerald, osa for locating the quotation and, along with Jane Albrecht, advising on its translation (here rather loose). For these and other quotations on the spirituality of nature, see the website www.creationethics.org and click on "historical writings." The site is part of "Opening the Book of Nature," a nationwide program of experiential learning.
4. *Nature Writings* (New York: The Library of America, 1997), 228. Cf. "mountain manuscripts," 288.
5. Perhaps the use of the verb "participate" suggests the *activity* of participating. Our very *use* of the word "nature" thus reflects our alienation from it. The problem also appears in the word "environment," which suggests what is outside of and around me

rather than a physical and spiritual reality within which I am an inextricable part.

6. Here we will be following the work of David Abram, *The Spell of the Sensuous* (New York: Random House, 1996). Abram focuses on that branch of the philosophy of language known as phenomenology (i.e., paying attention to the *phenomena* of experience), comparing it to the sensibilities of "oral, indigenous" cultures.

7. *Time*, Special Edition, Spring, 2001, 11–12.

8. *WH* 80, emphasis Oliver's.

Notes to Chapter 1: The Circuit of the Sun

1. David Abram, *The Spell of the Sensuous* (New York: Random House, 1996), 116–117. We will return to the significance of "participant" in Chapter 2. Cf. Oliver's use of "participate" as a noun discussed in the introduction.

2. *Ibid.*, 80–81. Moreover, "Even boulders and rocks seem to speak their own uncanny languages," 63.

3. Maurice Merleau-Ponty, quoted in *Ibid.*, 86. Cf. Mark I. Wallace, "The Wounded Spirit as the Basis for Hope in an Age of Radical Ecology," in *Christianity and Ecology*, ed. Dieter Hessel and Rosemary Radford Ruether (Cambridge: Harvard University Press, 2000), 58: "God as Trinity subsists in interpersonal unity through incarnating Godself in all things that swim, creep, crawl, run, fly, and grow upon the earth."

4. On the "now" in Oliver's poems, cf. also *TM* 52, 64.

5. However, such sayings often have produced the very problem that Oliver is addressing, a longing for "eternal life" that robs the present and this world of significance. At its worst, such interpretations of "eternal life" produce an anti-worldly view that is not even Christian (see the Epilogue). In the Gospel of John, for example, "eternal life" clearly involves life that death cannot destroy, but it also refers to a quality of life that is "given here and now." (See Raymond E. Brown, *The Gospel According to John, Vol. 1*, Anchor Bible Commentary [Garden City: Doubleday, 1966], 507.)

6. Referring to such parables on the realm of God, C. H. Dodd says that "there is no mere analogy, but an inward affinity, between the natural order and the spiritual order . . . , the kingdom of God is intrinsically *like* the processes of nature and the

daily life of men." (Quoted in George Henry, *Theology of Nature* [Philadelphia: Westminster, 1980], 63.)

7. However, it is possible that the entire Psalm refers only to the Other Book. Cf. James Barr, *Biblical Faith and Natural Theology* (Oxford: Clarendon, 1993), 115, who thinks that Psalm 19 breaks down the distinction between "natural" and "revealed" theology, and that vv 7-13 (the Torah part) may refer not to the written law but to nature when it speaks its own rules.

8. Hopkins's "God's Grandeur" is widely anthologized.

9. I have used this illustration in a discussion of the mediated word of God in *Deuteronomy* (Deuteronomy [Louisville: Westminster John Knox, 1995], 46-48).

10. As George Washington Carver said, "If you love it enough, anything will talk to you." For other examples of hearing voices in nature see K. C. Cole, *The Hole in the Universe* (New York: Harcourt, 2001), 111; David Brendan Hopes, *A Sense of the Morning* (New York: Simon & Schuster, 1988), 169, 199; Aldo Leopold, *A Sand County Almanac* (New York: Oxford, 1987 [1949]), 85, 149, 153.

11. *The Other Way to Listen*, by Byrd Baylor and Peter Parnall (New York: Charles Scribner's Sons: 1978), n.p. Another beautiful example of a child learning from his grandfather how to listen to nature is *Grandpa's Prayers of the Earth*, by Douglas Wood and P. J. Lynch (Cambridge, MA: Candlewick, 1999).

12. *Gravity and Grace* (Minneapolis: Augsburg, 1986), 21.

13. For an evangelical view, see Mark A. Noll, *The Scandal of the Evangelical Mind* (Grand Rapids: Eerdmans, 1994), 207-208. Noll quotes Charles Hodge: "Nature is as truly a revelation of God as the Bible," and suggests that we need "to read the book of Scripture and the book of nature together."

14. For a rigorous philosophical analysis of what it means to say that God speaks, see Nicholas Wolterstorff, *Divine Discourse*. Note especially the case study on pp. 274-280, involving a woman who received a "revelation" from God even though "there was no external voice." Cf. Walter Wink: "So we listen to the [biblical] text. But with whose voice does it speak? It is a text still, not a person. It has no voice of its own. 'Letting the text speak' is, after all, only a figure of speech. . . . The text is *mute!* [So we really operate on] the prior *assumption* . . . that something speaks through the text which called the text *and myself* into being. . . . In the text I hope to encounter an alien speech which is finally

the self-disclosure of God." (*The Bible in Human Transformation* [Philadelphia: Fortress Press, 1973], 74.).

15. Quoted by Ronald A. Simkins, *Creator and Creation* (Peabody, MA: Hendrickson, 1994), 130.

16. Dale Patrick, *The Rhetoric of Revelation in the Hebrew Bible* (Minneapolis: Fortress, 1999), 71.

17. Far from implying falsehood, this process (again, essentially metaphorical) is the only means to certain kinds of truth. Robert Alter suggests that prophetic poetry in the Bible is "fictive," involving "an implied element of 'as if'" God is speaking. (*The Art of Biblical Poetry* [New York: Basic Books, 1985], 141.) See also his *The Art of Biblical Narrative* (New York: Basic Books, 1981), especially chap. 2, "Sacred History and the Beginnings of Prose Fiction," and Walter Brueggemann, *Finally Comes the Poet* (Minneapolis: Fortress, 1989), especially the introduction, "Poetry in a Prose-Flattened World."

18. Or, as Rolf Knierim says, "the world order points to, and in this case 'reveals,' the divine creator." *The Task of Old Testament Theology* (Grand Rapids: Eerdmans, 1995), 203.

19. *The Spell of the Sensuous*, 130.

20. Cf. *Ibid.*, 42–43.

21. As many scientists now recognize, our failure to value nature's cyclical order appears in our wanton pursuit of "progress" and "development" to such an extent that we are changing the climate. As a result, we are altering bird migrations, melting glaciers, shifting drought and rainfall, raising sea levels, and a host of other changes. In effect, climate change is the ultimate act of hubris: we *humans* are creating a "new heaven and a new earth" (Isa 65.17; Rev 21.1). See J. R. McNeill, *Something New Under the Sun: An Environmental History of the Twentieth-Century World* (New York: W. W. Norton, 2000) with reference to Eccl 1.9.

22. TM 21; NSP 190. Cf. also the reference to "kingdoms" in TM 3, 73.

23. William Gay, *The Provinces of Night* (New York: Doubleday, 2000), 39. On the difference between historical and cyclical time, see *The Spell of the Sensuous*, 181, 185, 189, 194–195. Abram quotes Paul Shepard's observation: "the idea of history is itself a western invention whose central theme is the rejection of habitat" (181).

•:•

Notes to Chapter 2: Attitude

1. Ps 104.27–30; Eccles 3.19; cf. Gen 7.2 Significantly, in Gen 2.7 and 19, both humans and animals are called *nephesh hayyah*, but both the KJV and the NRSV obscure the common identity, the KJV rendering the two respectively as "living *soul*" and "living creature," the NRSV as "living *being*" and "living creature."

2. Lynn Margulis, "Talking on the Water," *Sierra* (May/June, 1994), 72. Cf. Larry L. Rasmussen, *Earth Community, Earth Ethics* (Maryknoll, NY: Orbis, 1996), 222: "The breath of life the trees breathe out, I breathe in," then including soil, birds, water. "And this [is the] mighty presence, the truly mighty God. . . ."

3. David Abram, *The Spell of the Sensuous* (New York: Random House, 1996), 226, 238.

4. *Ibid.,* 46.

5. On the connotations of "dirty" see the Epilogue. Humans come from the humus (Hebrew *'adam* and *'adamah*). The word for ground refers not to Earth (as planet) but to earth as tillable soil, an agricultural image. For the larger significance of this agricultural anthropology (and theology) see Theodore Hiebert, *The Yahwist's Landscape: Nature and Religion in Early Israel* (New York: Oxford, 1996).

6. Alienation is expressed by the curse on the earth or ground (3.17). Though this curse is lifted later (8.21), the mythic dimension of the story suggests a permanent loss of intimacy that will be restored only in death (3.19). Although Christian burial liturgies (and Ash Wednesday rituals) often quote the phrase "dust to dust" (Gen 3.19), burial *practices* often deny it. An embalmed body inside a sealed casket inside a sealed vault will not turn to dust, nor become food for other creatures. See below on death and resurrection, especially n. 52.

7. *Nature Writings* (New York: The Library of America, 1997), 233.

8. Cf. also Sallie McFague, *Super, Natural Christians* (Minneapolis: Augsburg, 1997), 26–29, and Douglas Burton-Christie, "Words beneath the Water: Logos, Cosmos, and the Spirit of Place," in *Christianity and Ecology,* ed. Dieter Hessel and Rosemary Radford Ruether (Cambridge: Harvard, 2000), 317–336, with some references to Oliver.

9. As quoted in Frederick and Mary Ann Brussat, *Spiritual Literacy* (New York: Scribner, 1996), 164.

10. Here we may note the distinction between "theophany," "epiphany," and "hierophany." Those are technical words that

have to do with the appearance (-phany) of the divine. Each word can have a different nuance. Theophany can refer to the appearance of God, i.e., a particular deity. Epiphany can mean the same thing, or it can refer not so much to an appearance of (a) God but to a profound discovery of meaning or understanding. Similarly, hierophany refers to the appearance of the sacred or the holy. Philosophically, all three terms could refer to a sense of connection with the very ground of being, with what is ultimately real (ontology).

11. *Genesis: A Bible Commentary for Teaching and Preaching* (Atlanta: John Knox, 1982), 36.

12. See also "Five A.M. in the Pinewoods," (*NSP* 70).

13. Quoted by Dorothee Soelle, *Suffering* (Philadelphia: Fortress, 1975), 77.

14. "Dogfish," (*NSP* 105); cf. "The Egret," p. 47.

15. See her discussion of this poem in *WH* 24–26.

16. *WH* 98, emphasis added; cf. especially "Stars" (*WW* 13).

17. *Nature Writings*, 161.

18. "Landscape" (*DW* 68; *NSP* 129); "First Snow" (*AP* 26; *NSP* 150); "Winter Trees" (*TM* 72).

19. Cf. Abram, *The Spell of the Sensuous*, 81, who refers to the "chattering, whispering, soundful depths" of nature's language.

20. *Ibid.*, 121.

21. *Ibid.*, 55.

22. We will return to the subject/object dichotomy in the next chapter. See Ian Barbour, *Religion in an Age of Science* (San Francisco: Harper & Row, 1990), 31–36; Mary Gerhart and Allan Russell, *Metaphoric Process: The Creation of Scientific and Religious Understanding* (Fort Worth: Texas Christian University, 1984), 20–25; Sallie McFague, *Super, Natural Christians* (Minneapolis: Augsburg, 1997), 7–9; Langdon Gilkey, *Nature, Reality, and the Sacred* (Minneapolis: Fortress, 1993), 17–33.

23. *The Spell of the Sensuous*, 38. "Intersubjectivity" has an interesting parallel in the Buddhist thought of Thich Nhat Hanh, who has coined the words "inter-are" and "inter-being": "'To be' is to inter-be. We cannot just be by ourselves alone. We have to inter-be with every other thing," *Peace is Every Step* (New York: Bantam, 1991), 95–96. Nhat Hanh's passage on "Flowers and Garbage" (96–98) also reminds us of Oliver's correlation of beauty and ugliness, e.g., in "Skunk Cabbage" (see next page).

•:•

24. Quoted by Matthew Fox, *Original Blessing* (Santa Fe, NM: Bear & Co., 1983), 132. The Christological paradigm appears in Philippians 2.7.

25. "The Sea," *AP* 69; "Spring," *HL* 6; "Winter Sleep," *TM* 53; and "The Egret," *NSP* 47, respectively. Compare how John Muir is "dissolved and absorbed" by the Sierra landscape in *Nature Writings*, 175.

26. "A Few Words," *BP* 92. See her description of a spider and its prey in *WH* 82.

27. *Ibid.*

28. *Ibid.*, 93. The same dethronement of humans seems to be in mind in "At Loxahatchie" (*DW* 84), where Oliver wanders in the lush garden with all sorts of creatures and her "place in this garden" is not to be the gardener, and "nothing / needed to be saved"; cf. also *WP* 35 and Muir, *Nature Writings*, 825–826. While it is difficult to escape the violent connotation of human "subduing" of the earth (Gen 1.26), human "dominion" need not be tyrannical—such dominion should mirror that of the creator, in whose image humans are made, and who shows immense care for the earth, declaring all of creation "very beautiful" (v 31).

29. *The Spell of the Sensuous*, 16.

30. Cf. Job on Leviathan: "Will you play with it as with a bird, or will you put it on leash for your girls?" (41.5). See Chapter 3.2 below.

31. Italics the author's. On the creation language, cf. Job 38.7.

32. Sallie McFague's *Super, Natural Christians*.

33. Cf. the end of "Ghosts" (*AP* 28; *NSP* 152), where Oliver asks a buffalo cow and calf if she can cuddle with them as a sign of their forgiveness for the way humans decimated their species.

34. *The Spell of the Sensuous*, 57.

35. Rosemary Radford Ruther, *Gaia and God*, (San Francisco: HarperSanFrancisco, 1992), 299, n. 5.

36. *Ibid.*, 235. For an extended discussion of the topic, see Gary Kowalski, *The Souls of Animals* (Walpole, NH: Stillpoint, 1999). Cf. the quotation from Wallace in Chap. 1, n. 3.

37. Oliver's poetry thus does not correspond to the critique of George Stuart Hendry, who complains that "the poetic celebration of nature" does not recognize "both the light and the dark" (*Theology of Nature* [Philadelphia: Westminster, 1980], 219).

38. "Winter Sleep" (*TM* 53); "Hunter's Moon—Eating the Bear" (*TM* 50; *NSP* 198); cf. also "Cold Poem" (*AP* 31).

∴

67

39. Humans can be both predator and victim. See "Farm Country" (*NSP* 211), where Oliver enters a henhouse for killing, but also "Mushrooms" (*NSP* 144), where the plant may be delicious but also may kill.

40. In her article on "The Language of Nature in the Poetry of Mary Oliver" (*Women's Studies* 21, 1992, 8), Diane S. Bonds suggests that Oliver is rejecting a "patriarchal" image of God. That may be, but the use of "He" is not sufficient to make the case. At least in her later poetry, Oliver is quite capable of referring to God as "he" in a non-pejorative way (*LC* 9, 50; *WK* 51-52). On "theological sadism," see Soelle, *Suffering*, 22-27.

41. Samuel E. Balentine, "For No Reason," *Interpretation* 57/4 (October, 2003), 358.

42. Bonds (see n. 40) also sees "a kind of crucifixion scene" here. On the other hand, according to my local seafood expert, the image may simply be that of a *hammerhead* shark, strung up by its tail, with the men standing on either side of their trophy holding one "hammer."

43. *A Grief Observed* (New York: Bantam Books, 1963), 35.

44. Ann & Barry Ulanov, *Primary Speech: A Psychology of Prayer* (Atlanta: John Knox, 1982), 66-67.

45. For a full discussion of storms, see chap. 4. Oliver's insistence that we accept both the brutality and the beauty of the world resembles Soelle's view that a genuine Christian acceptance of suffering "is an attempt to see life as a whole as meaningful and to shape it as happiness," *Suffering*, 108. The resultant understanding of evil and suffering resembles that of "radical suffering" and "The Ambiguous Creation" as discussed by Susan L. Nelson, "Facing Evil: Evil's Many Faces," *Interpretation* 57/4 (2003), 398-413.

46. "Little Owl Who Lives in the Orchard" (*NSP* 85). Note that its lace-framed face "could be a valentine"! Cf. also "The Black Snake" (*NSP* 184).

47. For other examples of reincarnation, see "Blossom" (*AP* 49), "Pink Moon—The Pond" (*TM* 7), "Bone Poem" (*TM* 46), "Moccasin Flowers" (*HL* 2), and "Wings" (*HL* 14).

48. Cf. Ruether, "Ecofeminism: The Challenge to Theology," in *Christianity and Ecology*, 108: "Lion and lamb do not lay down together but keep one another's population within sustainable limits by a bloody process of eating and being eaten."

49. *The Spell of the Sensuous*, 219, quoting Christopher Vecsey.

50. *Ibid.*, 219. See also Daniel Cowdin, "The Moral Status of Otherkind in Christian Ethics," in *Christianity and Ecology*, 285.

51. *Gaia and God*, 34. See also her "Ecofeminism," 104–106. See Paul Davies, *God and the New Physics* (New York: Simon & Schuster: 1983), 80f, 218f, who says that "the location of Heaven" has become "meaningless" in the context of modern cosmology yet leaves the question open.

52. *Ibid.*, 49. Cf. McFague, *The Body of God* (Minneapolis: Fortress, 1993), 176–177: "we do not have to leave God when we die, nor do we join God in heaven . . . , for whether our bodies are alive or return to the other form of embodiment from which they came, they are within the body of God," who is "with us in the earth, the soil, that receives us at our death." For a lyrical description of the soil as "the healer and restorer and resurrector" through the decay of bodies (except those embalmed and entombed!) see Wendell Berry, *The Art of the Commonplace* (Washington: Counterpoint, 2002), 30–31, 284. See also Richard Cartwright Austin, *Hope for the Land: Nature in the Bible* (Atlanta: John Knox, 1988), 225–226; Rasmussen, *Earth Community, Earth Ethics*, 277.

53. Daniel Cowdin, "The Moral Status of Otherkind in Christian Ethics," in *Christianity and Ecology*, 273. The entire article is an illuminating presentation of the larger issues. See the previous note also.

54. For other examples of how nature is "not pretty" see WP 4 and 49. On mud as the medium for transformation, see HL 40.

55. Paul Ricoeur, *The Symbolism of Evil* (Boston: Beacon, 1967), 351.

56. Alice Walker, *The Color Purple* (New York: Simon & Schuster, 1982), p. 179.

57. See LC 9–10, 49–50, 52–53; WK 51–52; OF 34.

58. WH 98–99. On the woods as temple, see Chap. 3.1, "The Blessing Tree."

59. *God in Search of Man* (New York: Farrar, Straus and Giroux, 1955), 45 and 74, emphasis the author's. Indeed, the sequence of chapter titles in Heschel's book provides a striking interpretive model here: "Ways to the Presence," "The Sublime," "Wonder," "The Sense of Mystery," "The Enigma is not Solved," "Awe," and "Glory."

60. *Ibid.*, 74, emphasis added.

1. Quoted in Charles Williams, *The Letters of Evelyn Underhill* (The Religious Book Club, 1945), 80.

2. Second Isaiah (Isaiah 40-55) uses numerous metaphors from nature: water, sprouting, stars, etc. While the references to trees "clapping their hands" surely suggest personification, it remains that the trees are celebrating the redemption of Israel from exile. In other words, here as elsewhere nature's role is to point to history. The trees do not celebrate just being trees. Similarly rivers, mountains, and wilderness areas are significant primarily because of what happens there, not because of what *is* there (e.g., Jordan River, Mt. Sinai, Negev wilderness).

3. A more "primitive" notion of a tree as speaking appears in the oak of Moreh (Gen 12.5-7). The word *moreh* derives from the word meaning "instruct" (as does the word "Torah"). This tree is an example of a layer of Israelite religion beneath the dominant historical focus (and largely ignored by scholars until recently). Here nature is "the realm through and within which God becomes present in the world," as Theodore Hiebert suggests in *The Yahwist's Landscape* (New York: Oxford University, 1996), 110.

4. Prv 3.18; cf. 11.30; 13.12; 15.4; Ps 1.3; Sir 24.8-22. Less abstract and probably closer to the original meaning of the tree is the reference to it in Gen 2.9; 3.22-24, where it offers the possibility of immortality. Similarly, the tree of life appears in eschatological and apocalyptic literature. In Ezek 47.7, 12, the new Jerusalem of the prophet's vision will include fruit trees that never wither and bear fruit all year long, as well as "leaves for healing." That imagery is continued in Rev. 2.7; 22.1-2, adding that only the faithful will have access to the tree of life. For a study on the symbolism of the sacred tree in ancient Israel see Carol L. Meyers, *The Tabernacle Menorah: A Synthetic Study of a Symbol From the Biblical Cult* (Missoula: Scholars Press, 1976), especially 140. The strict iconoclasm of the Deuteronomic reforms, fighting alleged Canaanite practices, condemned the use of trees as media for the sacred (Deut 16.21; 1 Kgs 14.23; 2 Kgs 16.4; Jer 2.27 [note also "stone"]).

5. A recent children's book pursues this symbolic tradition. In *The Tale of Three Trees*, by Angela Elwell Hunt (Colorado Springs: Lion Publishing, 1989), the three trees attain their true beauty (and utility) by becoming Noah's ark, Jesus' manger, and the cross.

6. "Easter" apparently was associated with the vernal equinox (and perhaps the goddess "Eostre")—that is, with natural cycles (and probably fertility) rather than historical events.

7. I quote from the second edition translated by Ronald Gregor Smith (New York: Charles Scribner's Sons, 1958). The following presentation of Buber's thought comes from pp. 7-8.

8. David Abram, *The Spell of the Sensuous* (New York: Random House, 1997), 38. "Trees . . . can seem to speak to us when they are jostled by the wind," and different species even have different dialects (129-130). Cf. Sallie McFague, *Super, Natural Christians* (Minneapolis: Augsburg, 1997), 30-39.

9. *Ibid.*, 45.

10. *Ibid.*, 54, 56. Cf. also Tilden Edwards, *Living in the Presence* (San Francisco: Harper and Row, 1987), 5: "if we are looking at a tree, in the instant before our reflective self appears to make some commentary on the tree, we are in a sense present 'in' the tree. No observer has risen to separate us 'out.'"

11. *Ibid.*, 9-10.

12. See Donald L. Berry, *Mutuality: The Vision of Martin Buber* (Albany: State University of New York, 1985), 18-19. For another analysis of the tree passage, see George Stuart Hendry, *Theology of Nature* (Philadelphia: Westminster, 1980), 202-203 (see also 36-39 on subject/object).

13. *The Spell of the Sensuous*, 248.

14. Cf. "Spring," AP 45, where the rain is "clean as holy water" and "rubs its shining hands all over me." John Muir talks about "Sierra manifestations of God" and quotes Emerson ("Come listen what the pine tree saith"), then says that the trees of Yosemite are the "high priests, the most eloquent and commanding preachers . . . stretching forth their century-old arms in benediction over the worshipping congregations crowded about them" (*Nature Writings*, 787).

15. In another remarkable musical exchange, Oliver plays Mahler for a mockingbird who then mimics the music (see HL 36). On holiness, see "At the Lake" (WP 18).

16. James McNeley as quoted by Abram, *The Spell of the Sensuous*, 233.

17. Rolf Knierim, *The Task of Old Testament Theology* (Grand Rapids: Eerdmans, 1995), 197. In this reticence, Oliver's work resembles the place of blessing within the wisdom tradition of the Hebrew Bible, where the presence of God is often hidden. What appears is the power of life itself.

•:•

18. *Farewell, I'm Bound to Leave You* (New York: Picador, 1996), 215 (emphasis added). Novelist and essayist Frederick Buechner offers an autobiographical analog to Oliver's experience of blessing by a tree. Buechner describes an encounter with a tree that was on his daily walk and which he had often touched as "a way of blessing it for being so strong and beautiful." But on one particular day he suddenly finds himself "touching it not to bless it for once, but to ask its blessing, so that I myself might move toward old age and death with something like its stunning grace and courage" (*The Longing for Home* [San Francisco: HarperSanFrancisco, 1996], 147). Indeed, Buechner goes on to say that the tree in this instance extends the saying of Jesus, "When I was a stranger, you welcomed me." That is, here in this encounter with a tree "Christ is risen and alive in the world."

19. Note that 38.8-11 makes reference to God's curtailment of the sea, probably referring to the mythic monster discussed below in Chap. 4.

20. See William P. Brown, *The Ethos of the Cosmos* (Grand Rapids: Eerdmans, 1999), 367. In the following, I am indebted to Brown's interpretation, especially of the wild animals.

21. On this interpretation, see the footnotes in the *HarperCollins Study Bible*. See also my essay "Job and *The Color Purple*," *Prism* 5/2, 1990, 70-71.

22. A phrase from Wendell Berry's poem "The Peace of Wild Things," *Collected Poems* (New York: North Point, 1984), 69.

23. Brown, *The Ethos of the Cosmos*, 367.

24. *Ibid.*, 368.

25. On the translation of "vulture" instead of "eagle," see Brown, *The Ethos of the Cosmos*, 364, n. 187.

26. A book by Belden C. Lane poignantly illustrates the way in which wilderness can provide comfort, as indicated in the title: *The Solace of Fierce Landscapes: Exploring Desert and Mountain Spirituality* (New York: Oxford, 1998). Lane's focus oscillates between his experiences in wilderness and the ordeal of his mother's death from cancer. Note his suggested exercise of sitting with an expanse of rock (168f), the very stability of which counters the instability of our lives: "The landscape's silent immensity—and the God to whom it points—is able to absorb all the grief one can give it."

27. *I and Thou*, 23, 11.

28. Cf. Gen 2.7, where God blew into the clay figure who then "became a living creature" (my translation).

29. Cf. her encounter with a deer in "The Pinewoods" (WP 13), and the total transformation described in "In Blackwater Woods" (WP 34).

30. Poems are about "passage" rather than "stasis," and the reader who enters the poem should "emerge a little different, forever, from what he or she had been before" ("The Poet's Voice," (BP 108-109). Oliver ends the essay with a poem by Rilke that concludes with an imperative: "You must change your life" (BP 115).

31. In "The Black Walnut Tree" Oliver describes how she and her mother decide not to turn the tree in their yard into lumber, despite their need to pay the mortgage (TM 56; NSP 201).

32. Philadelphia: Fortress Press, 1971.

33. Ibid., 68.

34. Opening the Bible (Philadelphia: Fortress Press, 1970), 27.

35. Ibid., 30.

36. Ibid., 71.

Notes to Chapter 4: Animate *Inanima*

1. See the end of Chap. 2 on Abraham Heschel's understanding of awe in religious experience.

2. The Idea of the Holy (New York: Oxford University Press, 1958 [1917]), 14.

3. In "Glorious Things of You Are Spoken," v 3. The imagery refers to the cloud and fire that sanctify the Tabernacle and Temple (Exod 40.34-38; 1 Kgs 8.10-13).

4. See my study Divine Presence and Guidance in Israelite Traditions (Baltimore: Johns Hopkins, 1977). On thunder as God's "voice" see above in Chapter 1 and note especially Psalm 29. For the phenomenological dimensions of the storm god, see David Abram, The Spell of the Sensuous (New York: Random House, 1997), 249.

5. Annie Dillard, Pilgrim at Tinker Creek (New York: Harper, 1974), 8.

6. Cf. the discussion of body/mind in the previous chapter, and see the Epilogue on the sensual.

7. Compare Howard Clinebell's description of his change from childhood fear of storms to adult exhilaration, Ecotherapy: Healing Ourselves, Healing the Earth (Minneapolis: Fortress, 1999), 203-204.

•:•

8. See also "Rain in Ohio" (*AP* 40; *NSP* 157), in which thunder-heads come on "dark hooves." Cf. Ps 18.9–14.

9. "The Waterfall" (*NSP* 19); "Hawk" (*NSP* 34–35).

10. *Time,* July 30, 2001, p. 36. Cf. "Sharks" (*TM* 33–34).

11. For the story see James B. Pritchard, ed., *Ancient Near Eastern Texts* (Princeton: Princeton University Press, 1969), 60–72. For recent studies see the references in Robert R. Wilson, "Creation and New Creation," in *God Who Creates,* William P. Brown and S. Dean McBride, Jr., eds. (Grand Rapids: Eerdmans, 2000), 191 and n. 4.

12. Pritchard, 72.

13. Jon Levenson (San Francisco: Harper and Row, 1988).

14. "The only argument there is / against the sea" (as death) is the hermit crab's occupation of the shell of a dead creature ("Hermit Crab," *HL* 10; *NSP* 74).

15. In "Serengeti" (*HL* 61), Oliver is amazed at "the terror and the awe" of a lion, "part of the idea of God." Cf. the mixture of fear and excitement over a copperhead in "May" (*HL* 5).

16. This movement is precisely that in Psalm 29.

17. The ancient dragon metaphor appears in the account of a surgeon who discovers a creature with pincers inside an abscessed wound in Richard Selzer, "The Art of Surgery," *Harper's,* Oct., 1975, as cited by Andrew Delbanco, *The Death of Satan* (New York: Farrar, Straus, and Giroux, 1995), 225–226.

Notes to Epilogue: Dirty Book

1. Cf. "Honey At The Table," *AP* 57, which traces a path from the honey pot on the table to the bee hive in the tree. Our ignorance of and detachment from the production of food is symptomatic of enormous environmental degradation. See the work of Wendell Berry, for example *The Art of the Commonplace: The Agrarian Essays,* Norman Wirzba, ed. (Washington, D.C.: Counterpoint, 2002), especially the closing essay, "The Pleasures of Eating." See also Bill McKibben, "Food Fight: Local Farming vs. Agribusiness," and the accompanying essay by H. Paul Santmire, "Farming for God," *The Christian Century,* 120/26, Dec. 27, 2003, 20–25. As McKibben says, "we have paid for our ignorance and indifference in diminished lives, lousy dinners and strained landscapes" (p. 22).

2. *Earth Community, Earth Ethics* (Maryknoll: Orbis, 1996), 239.

3. *Ibid.* Note also Rasmussen's argument that Luther was a panentheist, pp. 272–279. For other views on panentheism and sacramentalism, see Sallie McFague, *The Body of God* (Minneapolis: Fortress, 1993), 149f, 182–185 and *Life Abundant* (Minneapolis: Fortress, 2001), 141f, 169; Richard C. Austin, *Beauty of the Lord* (Atlanta: John Knox, 1988), 176–179 and *Hope for the Land* (Atlanta: John Knox, 1988), 179–189.

4. Rolf Knierim, *The Task of Old Testament Theology* (Grand Rapids: Eerdmans, 1995), 228. Cf. Paul Tillich, who favors the "realistic interpretation" of the Eucharistic bread and wine because (like the water of baptism) they are "representing the natural powers that nourish the body," and "they point to the presence of the divine saving power in the natural basis of all spiritual life," *The Protestant Era* (abridged ed.; Chicago: Phoenix Books, 1957), 96–98.

5. Quoted by Rasmussen, *Earth Community, Earth Ethics* (Maryknoll, NY: Orbis, 1996) , 278f. See also n. 3 above. The essay is entitled "That These Words of Christ—This is my Body, etc., Still Stand Firm against the Fanatics." Wendell Berry quotes lines from William Carlos Williams that refer to vegetables and seafood: "There is nothing to eat, / seek it where you will, / but of the body of the Lord," *The Art of the Commonplace, 327.*

6. *God the Economist: The Doctrine of God and Political Economy* (Minneapolis: Fortress, 1989), 179–180 (emphasis added). "Economy" and "ecology" derive from the same Greek word meaning "household." For the connection (along with ecumenicity) see Meeks, 34f.

7. David Abram, *The Spell of the Sensuous* (New York: Random House, 1996), 45. On Oliver's dissolution of patriarchal mind/body dualism, see Diane S. Bonds, "The Language of Nature in the Poetry of Mary Oliver," *Women's Studies* 21 (1992), 8.

8. Janet McNew calculates that sixteen poems in *American Primitive* "use eating as a central, eucharistic symbol"; "Mary Oliver and the Tradition of Romantic Nature Poetry," *Contemporary Literature* 30 (1989), 69.

9. In "The Sea," (*AP* 69; *NSP* 172) her Darwinian body remembers its life as a sea creature and longs to relinquish understanding for feeling.

10. It is a misinterpretation of Paul's use of "flesh" to see it simply as the material body. As Amos Wilder says, "Spirit and body are not antithetical in the thought of the Bible. The antithesis of

Spirit is flesh, and flesh is not un-spirited body; it is body in-spirited by another spirit, 'the spirit of the world,' as Paul calls it (1 Cor. 2:12)" (*Theology of Nature* [Philadelphia: Westminster, 1980], 169).

11. James B. Nelson, *Embodiment* (Minneapolis: Augsburg, 1978) 44.

12. See Paul Ricoeur, *The Symbolism of Evil* (Boston: Beacon, 1967).

13. Some representative examples are Mary Gerhart & Allan Russell, *Metaphoric Process: The Creation of Scientific and Religious Understanding* (Fort Worth: Texas Christian University, 1984); Ian Barbour, *Religion in an Age of Science* (San Francisco: Harper, 1990); Langdon Gilkey, *Nature, Reality, and the Sacred: The Nexus of Science and Religion* (Minneapolis: Fortress, 1993); McFague, *The Body of God*.

14. For the combination of body and spirit, see Genesis 2, where the "living being" is the *combination* of spirit (breath) and body (earth). Note also Ps 16.9: "my heart is glad, and my soul rejoices; my body ["flesh"] also rests secure."

15. "Where Is Your Soul, Anyway?" in *Spirituality and Health*, Fall, 1999, 25. The journal often addresses the integration of mind and body.

16. Rasmussen, *Earth Community*, 239; see also 273f; McFague, *The Body of God*, 183f and *Super, Natural Christians*, 102.

17. Elsewhere, the body is more dazzling than the spirit, willing to carry endless happiness (*AP* 62, 67).

18. Raymond Brown, *The Gospel According to John, Vol. 1* (Anchor Bible Commentary; Garden City: Doubleday, 1966), 31. It is interesting to compare this biblical model of incarnation with the thought of Merleau-Ponty. For him, "Flesh" refers not only to human beings but to the entire world. As Abram puts it, "The Flesh is the mysterious tissue or matrix that underlies and gives rise to both the perceiver and the perceived . . . the reciprocal presence of the sentient in the sensible and of the sensible in the sentient." Then he quotes Merleau-Ponty: "The presence of the world is precisely the presence of its flesh to my flesh." See *The Spell of the Sensuous*, 66, 69.

19. *The Spell of the Sensuous*, 65 (emphasis his). The term "life-world" is Husserl's. In Abram's words (p. 40), "The life-world is the world of our immediately lived experience, *as we live it*, prior to all our thoughts about it."

20. Tilden Edwards, *Living in the Presence* (San Francisco: Harper & Row, 1987), 47–48.

21. *Ibid.*, 52. Cf. the remark of Thomas Merton: "We are living in a world that is absolutely transparent, and God is shining through it all the time. . . . God shows Himself everywhere, in everything. . . . The only thing is that we don't see it." Quoted by Marcus Borg, *The Heart of Christianity* (San Francisco: HarperSanFrancisco, 2003), 155.

22. "A Certain Sharpness in the Morning Air" (*NSP* 41).